Mad Love for
MAD GENIUS

"Randy Gage is truly a genius—and entrepreneurs would be mad not to follow his stellar advice. Make your first mastermind alliance with this remarkable book."

—**Harvey Mackay**, author of the #1 *New York Times* bestseller *Swim with the Sharks Without Being Eaten Alive*

"A big and brave kick-start for anyone set to make their entrepreneurial dreams come true."

—**Robin Sharma**, #1 bestselling author of *The Leader Who Had No Title*

"This book is effin' great! Teaches not only a mindset, but gives you hope, inspiration, and challenges them at the same time. I love every part of it."

—**Larry Winget**, author of *Grow a Pair* and five other international bestsellers

"This life-changing book is loaded with practical, proven ideas and questions that will help you kick open the door to all the success you want." —**Brian Tracy**, author of *The Power of Self-Confidence*

"This is one of the messiest books I've ever read. I mean that in the best possible sense. Randy Gage takes us on Mister Toad's Wild Ride. I was hanging on for dear life. . . . It's a mad, mad, mad world inside Randy Gage's head—and I'm glad I took the trip."

—**Steven Pressfield**, bestselling author of *The War of Art* and *Turning Pro*

"*Mad Genius* is friggin' mind-rocking. It's a Vulcan mind meld between author and reader, where Gage exhibits what Mozart and Picasso did—artistry emerging from the riot within their own heads." —**Alan Weiss, PhD**, author of *Million Dollar Consulting*

continued . . .

"The title says it all: Randy Gage is both—mad and a genius!—and he puts it all in a book as a handbook for success!! CRAZY GOOD!"

—**Jeffrey Hayzlett**, prime-time TV show host, bestselling author, and sometime cowboy

"Brace yourself. You're about to be shaken and stirred by the insights, truths, and rip-roaring predictions of a mad wizard out to make you rich."   —**Joe Vitale**, author of *Attract Money Now*

"Only Randy Gage would challenge the conventional wisdom of everyone from Einstein to the Buddha—and lead you to conclude, 'Well, he does have a point!'"

—**Bob Burg**, coauthor of *The Go-Giver* and author of *Adversaries into Allies*

"Gage takes you places you really don't want to go but you need to go. He gives you the path to take the jump and create success like you've never imagined. There is truly 'madness in his method' and you will benefit from his genius."

—**Lisa Ford**, author of *Exceptional Customer Service*

"'Provocative' and 'practical' don't usually go together, but *Mad Genius* is both. It will stretch your thinking, challenge your beliefs, and then provide you things you can actually use to bring out your inner Mad Genius."

—**Mark Sanborn**, leadership adviser and bestselling author

"Most of us can accomplish so much more in life and *Mad Genius* is the roadmap to get us there. It's a bible for making big things happen. Do *yourself* a favor and read this book, nothing will look the same again."   —**Steve Keating**, author of the *LeadToday* blog

"This book shocks your system, challenges your assumptions, and opens your mind to radically new ways of thinking—and that's in just the first chapter! Gage is the master guide on the unorthodox path to entrepreneurial genius."

—**Rory Vaden**, *New York Times* bestselling author of *Take the Stairs*

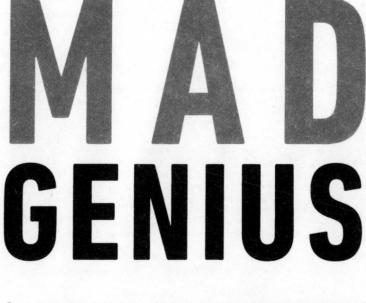

MAD
GENIUS

{ A MANIFESTO FOR ENTREPRENEURS }

RANDY GAGE

A PERIGEE BOOK

PERIGEE
An imprint of Penguin Random House LLC
375 Hudson Street, New York, New York 10014

MAD GENIUS

Library of Congress Cataloging-in-Publication Data

Gage, Randy, author.
Mad genius : a manifesto for entrepreneurs / Randy Gage.—First edition.
pages cm
ISBN 978-0-399-17556-5 (hardback)
1. Creative ability in business. 2. Creative thinking. 3. Entrepreneurship. I. Title.
HD53.G34 2016
658.4'063—dc23
2015031373

First edition: January 2016

PRINTED IN THE UNITED STATES OF AMERICA

1   3   5   7   9   10   8   6   4   2

Text design by Spring Hoteling

While the author has made every effort to provide accurate telephone numbers, Internet addresses, and other contact information at the time of publication, neither the publisher nor the author assumes any responsibility for errors, or for changes that occur after publication. Further, the publisher does not have any control over and does not assume any responsibility for author or third-party websites or their content.

Most Perigee books are available at special quantity discounts for bulk purchases for sales promotions, premiums, fund-raising, or educational use. Special books, or book excerpts, can also be created to fit specific needs. For details, write: SpecialMarkets@ penguinrandomhouse.com.

CONTENTS

PREFACE

{A Humiliating Confession}

What is it about genius that tortures so many who possess it? A Mad Genius if ever there was one, Hunter S. Thompson was asked how he created his unique brand of brilliance. His reply was inspired, if a little unnerving: "I hate to advocate drugs, alcohol, violence, or insanity to anyone, but they've always worked for me."

I wish I could say the muse for this book was a sudden inspiration of genius, but it was actually germinated in an environment of shame and wretched despair.

Shame because I was lying around my apartment, trying to throw off the aftereffects of a binge relapse with crystal meth—an addiction I had thought was long conquered.

And despair because the euphoria of the high (which gets less euphoric every time) was replaced by the exhaustion, nausea, and depression of the crash. Among meth addicts, these days are called "suicide Tuesdays" for reasons you can probably imagine.

Now if you think that seems like a less-than-opportune environment to foster creative genius, you're only half right. Because sometimes it is when we are at our lowest state, facing our most difficult challenges, that we pull ourselves together, marshal our resources, and decide that the alternative to hopelessness is actually hope after all.

You'll find this as a recurring theme in this manifesto: Why no is never the answer, failure isn't final unless you quit, and how challenges offer the greatest opportunities for innovation and creation.

Obviously this relapse was one more chapter of the twisted hero's journey my subconscious mind felt necessary to create for myself—to overcome my own insecurities and worthiness issues.

The good news is that I really believe this won't happen again. Sometimes you just know when you're done. I felt that way after I took my last drink on my twentieth birthday, and thirty-five years later, have never had the desire for another one. And just as I felt my life worked better without alcohol in it, I now feel that recreational drug use doesn't enrich my life but destroys it. So I chose life.

But I also had that unnerving pang . . .

Could I still write or would the goddess of creativity abandon me at the altar? Would I still possess the gift to recognize opportunities and build entrepreneurial ventures?

I grew up watching creative geniuses like Joplin, Hendrix, and Morrison blaze brilliantly, then die of overdoses. And I idolized writers like Hemingway, Poe, Kerouac, O. Henry, and Thompson, who all viewed drugs and alcohol as necessary ingredients for their creative genius—or at least helpful to medicate the issues preventing them from achieving it.

Fortuitously, I read *On Writing*, the brilliant memoir of the craft from Stephen King, who recounted his ability to face down his own addiction demons and still create. I began to think a look at genius—and how we harness, nurture, and direct it—would make a fascinating book. And even more intriguing, would be an exploration specifically of how the mindset of the entrepreneurial genius works.

As I was reading up on the links between creativity and mental illness, I found a Wikipedia entry that stated, "Psychotic individuals are said to display a capacity to see the world in a novel and original way, literally, to see things that others cannot."

Now, entrepreneurs are not psychotic, of course. We simply display a capacity to see the world in a novel and original way, literally, to see things that others cannot.

Oh, wait . . .

As entrepreneurs, we're hardwired to shake things up, live by our own set of rules, and, most importantly, create new things. Our greatest genius comes in the creation part.

That's the reason we watched the Steve Jobs product launches with breathless anticipation, we care more about the commercials than the Super Bowl, and we're almost giddy when we come across a Kickstarter campaign for a sexy new gadget. We're witnessing genius in action.

I pondered all this while watching *Before Night Falls*, the magnificent film that was based on the stunning book by Reinaldo Arenas. One genius showcasing the gifts of another. When you're exposed to a film or book like these, you can't help but want to create something amazing. Something that makes a difference.

So this manifesto comes to you from one of the lowest points in my life but, I hope, leads us both to reaching something much higher: harnessing your Mad Genius—and sharing it with the world. I hope you'll join the discussion on social media, using the hashtag #MadGenius.

You'll find this manifesto divided into three sections: Book One is a look at how we got to where we are now. How the convergence of bad premises, negative memes, and herd thinking infected our consciousness and allowed us to accept mediocrity. Book Two explores some of the earth-shattering, cataclysmic developments we will be facing in the upcoming decade. We'll peek around the corner, predict the future, recognize the inherent challenges in that future—which will reveal to us the greatest opportunities. And finally, Book Three is a chaotic collection of mind-bending, thought-provoking ideas to force you to think about what you think about. Read whatever section you need at the point you need it. But know that there is one constant in all three sections: the real-world truth about how you have to think to become a successful entrepreneur.

Inspirational business book authors may claim to play different tunes, but most of them are singing the same song of ever-growing success. The case studies all seem to follow the same template: A couple college kids with nothing but empty beer cans and pizza boxes littering their dorm rooms have a big idea. They drop out of school, set up shop, and become an overnight viral sensation. They get to choose from a swarm of VC investors who desperately want to throw money at them, ignore calls from Zuckerberg, float an IPO, become billionaires, and grace the cover of *Wired*.

Preface

Some of the readers who buy those books must wonder what they're doing wrong. In the real world of business, though, there are both breathtaking breakthroughs and soul-wrenching failures. It's a world with fears and doubts, sweating to make payroll, scrambling to raise money, struggling to stand out. I'm here to tell you that getting on top and staying on top is never a sure thing. But if you're willing to do the work and pay the price—success is attainable. It's never easy, but it's worth it.

—Randy Gage
San Diego, California

MAD
GENIUS

BOOK ONE

The MYSTERIOUS PEOPLE and the
SECRET SYSTEM THAT RUNS THE WORLD

Put yourself in this picture:

We were on Mo'orea, in French Polynesia (often known as the Tahitian Islands), at a luxury resort where the bungalows are suspended over the water with a hatch in the floor so you can feed the fish underneath. There were ten of us seated around a conference table loaded with tropical fruit, fresh-squeezed juice, and coffee. The morning sun was streaming in, the weather was sublime, and the environment was perfect for a brilliant brainstorming session.

The other nine people had paid $15,000 each and flown thousands of miles to have a three-day mastermind retreat with me. I began the session by going around the table, asking everyone to summarize the one big concept they would like to strategize during the retreat.

The first guy said he wanted to do a complete makeover of his website. The second person said she needed help with a title for her next book. The third person mentioned that he wanted some input on his next direct-mail campaign. It went on like this until it came back around to me. But before we go any further, if you really were around that table in Mo'orea right now—what would *you* say? Take a minute and really think about it.

Because here's what happened next.

I closed my eyes, took a slow, deep breath, and said, "I'm going to the fucking pool now. When you guys decide you want to actually have a mastermind and go after a *big* idea, then somebody come and get me."

Not sure what was said next, but after about ten minutes, one sheepish attendee came out and asked if I would rejoin the group.

So what happened?

Herd thinking happened. Like so often occurs in many situations, the person going first set the tone and everyone who followed unthinkingly shadowed the pattern. Of course, the interesting dynamic in this case was that these nine people were not random souls picked up at the bus stop. They were all hyper-successful, multimillionaire entrepreneurs who had invested a lot of money and time to be there to discover their next breakthrough.

You probably think they wouldn't fall prey to such disempowering thinking. But how did you reply to the question above? Was your answer really a big, bold, and breathtaking concept you wanted to mastermind on—or did you also default to some mundane tactic?

Even high achievers are not immune to being infected with herd thinking when they're members of a group. You'll see the same scenario if you start a meeting by asking people to go around the room giving their name and title, so everyone knows who's who. If the first person says, "Aldo Gonzalez, VP of quality control," everyone follows suit, your objective is accomplished, and you get down to work.

However, if the first person says, "Thanks, it's so great to be here. My name is Mary Marcus and I flew here from the Toronto division. My hobbies are embroidery and stamp collecting, and I'm really excited to be at this conference because I was just telling my sister last week that . . ."—you immediately know you're screwed. The intros you budgeted for five minutes will actually eat up twenty-five minutes of the ninety minutes you have.

The herd doesn't always follow the leader. Sometimes they simply follow whoever speaks first.

These examples illustrate a very important lesson about our thought processes, showing how we often go on autopilot and waste the amazing brainpower we possess.

In the case of the South Pacific retreat, the first person made a mistake in his thinking—a mistake many other entrepreneurs fall prey to: believing success to be about the tactics. But the genuinely important stuff is never about the tactics—it's actually about the big idea. When you get the big idea right, the tactics become readily apparent.

To truly harness your Mad Genius, you have to resist the urge to begin with tactics. You must first step back and do some critical thinking: What is the desired outcome here? Who is the real target market? What are the actual benefits for the people in the target group? What's the big idea? What is the story that will communicate the big idea?

Very few entrepreneurs and, shockingly, even very few large, successful companies take the time to really do this. For evidence, look no further than the literally billions of examples of horrible marketing we churn out, week after week.

No matter what kind of business you're in—sales and marketing are the engines that drive it. Every entrepreneur (and every manager who wants to think like an entrepreneur) has to at least be cognizant of what good marketing is and isn't. Yet it's alarming how many entrepreneurs—many of whom are bright, bold, and innovative—lose their ability for critical thinking, discernment, and even rationality when it comes to marketing. Many are totally ignorant of the subject, fobbing it off on someone else in their organization, if they are able to, or else an outside ad agency, hoping for the best.

The amount of dull, ineffective, and just plain ridiculous advertising out there is mind-numbing. Even worse, the biggest offenders are some of the largest brands in the world. You would think with huge creative teams and even bigger budgets, they'd be delivering a compelling, benefit-centered message, targeted to their best prospects. But if I have learned one universal truth about marketing, it is this:

The bigger the budget, the more stupid shit will be green-lighted.

A perfect example of this is beer advertising. A massive market, with billions of dollars spent in this category. Which means you'll see some of the most insipid, off-target, and downright wasteful advertising anywhere. (Although you have to give Anheuser-Busch creative points for having the chutzpah to promote themselves as "America's local brewery," since these days the multibillion-dollar conglomerate is actually owned by Belgian company InBev.)

We don't want to scan a code to see who was working on the assembly line the day our beer was bottled. And if your unique selling proposition is a wide hole in the top of the can—you probably should go back to the well and try again. Likewise if you think the most exciting thing about your beer is that I can punch an extra hole in the can with a can opener so the beer flows faster. Seriously? Can you imagine sitting in on the creative meeting where the big idea for the campaign was one of these?

Or how about the meeting where they had the brilliant concept to shape the can like a keg? And how many beer drinkers do you think were lying awake at night, wishing their beer can would change colors to tell them if it was cold? Can't you tell that when you're holding it?

All of these multimillion- and multibillion-dollar campaigns miss the mark because they were created with a tactical approach instead of first finding the big idea. And, of course, when you're really brilliant, the big idea will be centered not around the amazing features of your product or service but around the amazing benefits it provides the customer.

It's just human nature that when we're asked to market something, we default to listing its features. If I give you a widget to sell, it seems logical to describe its color, its size, and the materials it's made of. But do that and you've fallen prey to herd thinking. No one really cares about the features of your drill bit; they just want a hole in their wall.

You have to go the next step and think about exactly what the widget will do for the prospect: the delightful joy it will bring her when she gets it or the cataclysmic consequences she will suffer if she doesn't buy it.

The big idea should be the thing that grabs attention, attracts the tribe, or speaks directly to the prospect, but in the context of the benefit to her.

It should be the mechanism in the copy platform that pulls things together, creates the story arc, and pulls the prospect through the message to reach the desired conclusion.

It's great if you have Kevin Durant in your Sprint commercial. But with no big idea, it's just him talking to a goofy kid in a tree house dream sequence and has no relation to the message of the campaign. It's almost as pointless as the millions of dollars that beef jerky company spent on their nonsensical "messing with Sasquatch" commercials.

The fact your car has a push-button start is not a big idea to base a campaign on. Neither is the fact that your minivan has a foot-activated hatch. These hint at potential benefits, but they're still just minor features and certainly not important enough to base entire campaigns on, which several automakers have done.

Going back to Sprint, over the last few years they've had some of the craziest and questionable advertisements as any major brand. Remember those commercials with James Earl Jones and Malcolm McDowell dramatizing text messages? The first one was clever and showed some potential. But then they got downright creepy. And *creepy* is way too kind a word to describe the "framily" campaign they were running as I was writing this, featuring a family with a French-speaking daughter and a father played by a gerbil in a fishbowl with a Yiddish accent. WTF! What I wouldn't have given to be in that creative meeting and hear the logic behind that.

Sometimes the big idea is little.

I was working out at my gym the other day when I noticed one of the physical therapists there had set up his massage table in the middle of the gym and leaned a whiteboard against it, where he had written simply:

TELL ME WHAT HURTS

How's that for intriguing the prospect, grabbing attention, and creating a compelling headline?

Turns out his name is Ryan and he specializes in assisted myofascial release. I asked what it could do for my herniated disc, hoping to prolong my legendary (in my own mind at least) softball career. Ryan suggested he might be able to release some tension around the disc that was causing pain to radiate down my legs and offered to test some techniques on me. He did a ten-minute treatment, after which I immediately signed up for a series of five sessions at $95 each.

You may be thinking that Ryan's whiteboard and free sample idea won't scale for a big business like yours. But I bet with a little critical thinking you could find a way to adapt something similar. (And I'll wager Ryan booked more real business as a result of his zero-cost, two-hour campaign than Sprint booked with $5 million worth of their talking gerbil commercials.) Even if you can't replicate what Ryan did, you can build your marketing around a prospect-centered, benefit-driven platform. And you can have a big idea or theme that pulls everything together.

Of course, marketing is just one of many areas in which you can fall victim to herd thinking. It's just as easy to disengage your critical thinking gear when evaluating potential markets, assessing new opportunities, and developing innovative products and in lots of other areas. The good news is once you really develop your Mad Genius, you'll stop falling into habitual thinking and always approach every situation as a critical thinker, seeing possibilities instead of believing in . . .

THE BIG LIE

Ask any hundred people what the opposite if success is, and ninety-nine will probably answer, "Failure." But that's the big lie.

The real opposite of success is not failure but mediocrity.

Not only is failure *not* the opposite of success, *it is actually an integral and necessary element of success.* There has never been a goal worthy of achieving that didn't warrant some failures along the way. In fact, the greater the chance and degree of failure, the more astonishing any potential achievement can ultimately be.

Failures are not dead-end outcomes. (Unless you quit, and then you've ended the story.) The entrepreneur who doesn't make mistakes doesn't make anything. The fastest way to a disruptive breakthrough today is experimentation and failing fast.

Failures are simply momentary challenges. When you persevere through them, these challenges become the stepping-stones to your success. They allow you to learn lessons, modify strategies, and develop the necessary character to become a successful entrepreneur.

The other big misconception about entrepreneurial success concerns money. Or more precisely, the lack of it. Many studies show the biggest cause of business failure is undercapitalization. And most entrepreneurs bemoan their inability to get financing and attract investors. But in reality, no one has a money shortage. *What they really suffer from is an idea shortage.*

There are billions of dollars, pounds, pesos, euros, and rubles all over the world desperately looking for projects to invest in, causes to support, and solutions to buy. The only thing between you and the money you're seeking or the outcome you wish to create is the right idea.

So this is a manifesto about ideas. Big ideas, small ideas, and outlandish ideas. Ideas that innovate, ideas that disrupt markets, and especially ideas that irritate.

Deeper than ideas, though, this book is about how ideas are born and the role they play in entrepreneurial thinking. And the kinds of thinking that will be required from both you and me, as we enter the most exciting time in human history. We'll explore conventional thinking, logical thinking, lateral thinking, and creative thinking and how we mix them all together to create Mad Genius.

This is a manifesto for managers who want to become leaders and leaders prepared to lead in an age of exponential disruption. Because whether you work in a traditional business, run a nonprofit service organization, or are a government official managing a department, the best way to create fresh and innovative solutions is to think like an entrepreneur. Which is where we will begin.

CREATING ART

Entrepreneurship is artistry, because we create entities that have never existed before. Like all true artists, we don't create our art for the money or the fame, *we create our art because we have to.* We have no problem becoming the next dot-com billionaire gracing the cover of *Fast Company*, but we'd do what we do whether it made us rich or not. There is a void in our psyche that can be filled only when we are solving challenges, designing solutions, developing products, opening markets, innovating processes, and creating jobs.

This is a yearning that not all people feel. In fact, most don't. Most people who go to work are happy to fit in, look competent, and not get fired. When they set out to create something—whether it's a pizza parlor, a sci-fi screenplay, or a boutique advertising agency—they try their hardest to fit in with the others in their space.

True entrepreneurs, and the visionary employees who think

like them, aren't interested in following the pack. They have to lead the pack. Not for ego or status. Simply because they can't operate any other way.

Ultimately, this manifesto is a call for leadership, for new and fresh ideas on the way we create art. More specifically, it's a call to develop a thinking process that produces the disciplines of art we call innovation, market disruption, breakthrough products, brilliant marketing, industry reinvention, and iconic branding.

It will require that you go outside yourself and become the thinker of the thought—recognizing, analyzing, and quantifying the cognitive process that successful entrepreneurs use to create the outcomes that only we can create. It takes the mindset of possibility, of never saying no, and of being open to where the art takes us.

It is a lesson I learned personally from the Mad Watchmaker.

Back in the 1990s I was conducting a business congress in central Europe with Nicolas Hayek, the rumbustious founder of the Swatch Group. At the time, Hayek was probably in his mid-seventies, had singlehandedly rescued the entire Swiss watch industry, and was a billionaire at least four times over. Not that any of that had mellowed him any.

We were conducting a press conference to promote the event when a young reporter asked Hayek when he was planning on retiring. Hayek looked at him as though the man had called his mother a whore. Then in his gruff, irascible style, he proclaimed:

"ENTREPRENEURS ARE ARTISTS. AND ARTISTS NEVER RETIRE!"

At that very moment, I was struck by two fundamental truths.

One, I knew I would spend the rest of my life wishing I had been the first person in the world to utter those words.

And two, I now had a label to define my angst. (Hayek never did retire, by the way. He died unexpectedly of cardiac failure while busy at work in the Swatch corporate headquarters in 2010.) I had tried to retire once when I was forty and had my first midlife crisis. I thought I would do nothing but play softball, race cars, and drink out of coconuts. That lasted nine months. The inactivity drove me crazy so I got back in the game. I never understood why I needed to be back in the game. But the instant Hayek made his declaration, I knew.

THE ENTREPRENEUR AS ARTIST

Seth Godin's book *The Icarus Deception* is a brilliant take on the role of artistry in being an entrepreneur. And Steven Pressfield's magnificent book, *Turning Pro: Tap Your Inner Power and Create Your Life's Work*, also offers some great insights into the fascinating intersection of creative genius and the everyday work world. One fundamental truth that underscores both books is that entrepreneurial artists don't solve problems as much as they reveal or create possibilities. (More about this in a bit.)

Think of all the memes we have circulating about art: from starving artist to writer's block, from appreciated only after death to tortured genius. The parallels with entrepreneurs are many.

Like the writer hunched over a keyboard, staring at the

flashing cursor, an entrepreneur trying to make a payroll might occupy the loneliest place on earth. Admittedly, entrepreneurs won't usually cut off an ear like Van Gogh did. We're much more neurotic than that.

Having a dream. Raising capital. Employee issues. Doubt from family and friends. Getting to market. The market yawning. Employee issues. Skepticism from your peers. Making payroll. Product development. Employee issues. Growing pains. Jealousy from family and friends. Attacks from the media. Branding concerns. Cash flow problems. Employee issues. Inventory nightmares. Government regulation. Did I mention employee issues?

It takes vision to see something that hasn't been invented yet. It takes guts to go after that vision in the face of doubt, criticism, and even ridicule. It takes resiliency to stay the course in meager times. Being an entrepreneur requires a mindset that few possess because bringing a concept to market is as much an emotional rollercoaster as writing *For Whom the Bell Tolls*, sculpting *David*, or composing *La Bohème*.

SEE THE INTANGIBLE

When something has never existed before, it's not uncommon for it to be misunderstood, misinterpreted, and misconstrued. If you come upon a mother of dragons speaking Dothraki and you've never encountered such a thing before, your inability to correctly process what is in front of your eyes can deceive you. This misguided perception can cause you to miss opportunities or even sabotage your own success.

How do you describe chocolate to someone who has never tasted it, explain green to a blind person, or depict Mötley Crüe to a deaf one? You might have an easier time trying to explain reincarnation to a giraffe.

There was a time when Amazon was a ridiculous idea—until the moment it became a brilliant one. There was a time when MySpace was a concept of genius—until it became a flop—and perhaps could become something significant again. Facebook was a hit, then a dud, then took over the world. At least for now.

Innovation and other breakthrough ideas come about from a higher level of thinking than problem solving or even anticipating trends. Innovation and true breakthrough concepts come about only when we have the courage to go back to a blank canvas and envision a reality that has never existed before. This is Mad Genius. This is never saying no and seeing only possibilities.

The Dodge Viper was created from a dramatically higher level of thinking than the Chrysler K car was. It's a form of thinking that isn't taught in MBA programs and you don't find in many C-suites. Unfortunately, both the academic and corporate environments are chiseled into reactive, backward-looking thinking.

You can't get to where you want to go by thinking that way. You've got to escape herd thinking and unleash your Mad Genius.

I get that you're not like most people. You wouldn't have picked up this manifesto if you were. Yet I seriously doubt you are aware of the awesome magnitude of innate genius you already possess. You've bought into the lies, limiting beliefs, and negative memes.

YOU SETTLED

You believe that other people have genius, and you are just you. But if I've learned anything in twenty-five years of working with leaders, it is this: Everyone has the gift of genius. Including you. But genius is not something you find; it is a process you develop. It's a circuitous, mysterious, and often unsettling process. So I'm here to unsettle you.

DECIDE WHERE TO RESIDE

Mad Genius starts with a decision. The decision to tap your genius is about thinking in new and different ways. It happens when you refuse to accept no and decide to find a way. Even when there isn't a way.

Mad Genius also is dramatically affected by the neighborhood you choose to hang out in. Not the street you live on, but the region where you park your mind. And try as you might, you can't live in two places at once. Here are the possibilities:

Mediocrity. This is where most people live. There's a serious overpopulation issue here.

Good. Less populated but still very crowded. No one will criticize you for living here. In fact, most of your neighbors will graciously welcome you to the neighborhood and encourage you to stay.

Great. Real estate values are high in this neighborhood. Lots of people want to live here, but few actually do.

Mad Genius. This is the place where the elite artists in any profession hang out. It's a members-only club, but there's no invitation. You qualify for the club just because you decide to. You knock on the door of opportunity, and if it doesn't answer—you kick in the goddamned door.

THE PRICE YOU PAY

If you want to tap into the innate brilliance you possess and lead an organization that produces Mad Genius results, you have to be willing to take risks. And be willing to fail. And I'm not talking about third-quarter results off by a few percentage points. I'm talking about doing something everyone says you can't do, and then having everyone watch you not do it. Because even an epic failure—as painful as that is—lets you know you're in the game and playing at a world-class level.

Steve Jobs is idolized for being an innovative, creative genius, and he certainly was. But don't forget the serious failures and missteps he had along the way. In reality, it was his willingness to fail that ultimately led him to succeed at such breathtaking levels.

Did you know that when Jobs died, he was the single largest shareholder of Disney? That's where his greatest wealth came from, not Apple. After he was fired from Apple in 1985—something that was probably the right decision, from Apple's point of view—one of the two companies he founded was Pixar. It took Pixar nearly a decade to bring out its first film, the first all digitally animated film, but its eventual sale to Disney made him more than just a board member. It made him a billionaire.

If you want to do something epic, you must be willing to face challenges, some of which will temporarily defeat you. But those challenges are the stepping-stones that help you modify your strategies, gain new knowledge, and develop the character traits required to become great.

No one ever had a momentous breakthrough in their comfort zone, and you won't be the first. Be willing to pay the price.

WHO PICKED SALT AND PEPPER?

Why are salt and pepper the two seasonings available in almost every restaurant and dinner table in the Americas? Why not sea salt, paprika, or chili powder? And why just two choices, and not three or five?

WHO SAYS THE NORTH POLE IS ON THE TOP?

Most people seem to think so. But looking from my apartment in Sydney, I can tell you for certain that the South Pole is definitely on top. In actuality, the top is relative to what angle you're viewing the earth from the galaxy.

WHAT IF EINSTEIN WAS WRONG?

Probably the most quoted statement from Albert Einstein is the quip defining insanity as doing the same thing, yet expecting different results. But, of course, Socrates cautioned us about believing everything we read on the Internet.

That insanity quote actually came out of a Narcotics Anonymous pamphlet published more than thirty years ago and has been attributed to lots of people ever since, including Einstein. And while it was great advice back then, or even until recently, it no longer is.

THE RULES HAVE CHANGED

Today's marketplace changes by the second. The entire world is in constant change. Doing the same thing and expecting to get the *same* results today is insane. Yet most entrepreneurs and companies are still locked into the old paradigm. Today's fast-shifting, technology-driven world requires doing new and different things.

And the only way to change the way you do things is to change the way you think about them.

No matter what field you're in, there always seems to be a usual way of doing things, accepted practices, and conventional beliefs. But how often are conventional beliefs simply an excuse to avoid the really difficult work of critical thinking?

Instead of following accepted premises, you've got to question them. Doing this expands the bandwidth of your brain to be open to think in new and different directions. There are millions of people who can tell you why something won't work. You have to discover how it can.

The greatest killer of creativity and innovation is our predisposition to want to keep things the way they are. We like things known to us and comfortable. And, of course, we can be stymied because "That's the way it's always been done."

But when you leave something the same, you're actually subjecting it to a great deal of change. Paint a fence white and leave it alone, and it will turn gray over time. Leave it long enough, and it will end up black.

No object (or policy, method, or best practice) operates in a vacuum. Even things left alone are subject to the influences of the changing environment around them. Volcanoes create new islands, markets adjust, muscles atrophy, earth settles, relationships change, economies adjust, and people die.

The average age of companies on the original Fortune 500 list in 1955 was seventy-five years. Today, the average age is ten. Ten years from now I expect it to be fewer than five. Even the most brilliant idea becomes obsolete if left static long enough. So the real questions to consider are these: What other conventional wisdom have you automatically accepted because they said it was so? And who the hell are "they" anyway?

As an entrepreneur, you have to change the default setting you've probably been programmed with (No, that won't work) and reset it to a new mindset (*never say no*). The amount of deprogramming that requires this cannot be underestimated. Which takes us to the real identity of "they."

The MYSTERIOUS PEOPLE in Charge of the SECRET SYSTEM THAT RUNS THE WORLD

You are probably wondering, "Who are these mysterious people, and how does this system eviscerate innovation, freethinking, and common sense?" The story begins simply enough in the taxi stand at London's Heathrow Airport.

Peter, the cab driver who ended up getting my fare, had been waiting in the taxi lot for almost two hours. I, along with almost a hundred other people, had been standing in the aforementioned taxi stand in the bone-chilling London weather for more than twenty minutes, waiting for a cab.

Perhaps you're pondering why I and millions of other travelers who land at Heathrow have to endure this wait in the frigid UK winter. The reason is that the MYSTERIOUS PEOPLE in charge of the SECRET SYSTEM THAT RUNS THE WORLD who designed the taxi stand system at Heathrow decreed it to be so. Here's how the system works:

One employee is hired to stand at the front of the queue and instruct people to wait until there are at least forty people freezing in the cold. Another employee is hired to walk back and forth in front of the line receiving abuse from irate, cold people who are wondering why they don't call some taxis. The first employee then radios for four taxis to arrive from the five hundred that have been idling for hours at the airport, waiting for a fare.

The first employee instructs the cold people to wait. The second employee walks along the cabstand and verifies that the four taxis that have arrived are actually taxis. Then employee one asks the first party in line where they are going and directs them to cab one. He does the same for the second, third, and fourth parties, directing each one to a cab. The second employee walks up and down the line, receiving abuse from the irate, cold people who are wondering why they don't call some more taxis.

The line of cold people has now grown to more than a hundred. Employee one radios for four more taxis from the five hundred that have been idling for hours at the airport, waiting for a fare, and the process repeats, over and over, until 4 a.m., when the line dwindles down to nothing . . .

. . . *and then it starts all over again.*

Perhaps you think this process is counterproductive and dysfunctional. Perhaps you think it could be facilitated much more simply. But then you would be questioning the MYSTERIOUS PEOPLE in charge of the SECRET SYSTEM THAT RUNS THE WORLD. More about that in a minute.

When I finally make it to the front of the queue, employee one asks me where I am going and directs me to cab one, which happens to be driven by Peter. He admits that he is frustrated at having to wait two hours to get a fare, but he has resigned himself to accepting the status quo, no doubt because it is dictated by the SECRET SYSTEM THAT RUNS THE WORLD.

Now perhaps you're thinking that this taxi system is an anomaly because it is likely designed by government bureaucrats who would think in a way diametrically opposite to entrepreneurial and creative thinking. And you believe such an instance could never take place in the free enterprise environment. But what happened next when I arrived at my London hotel proves the depth of this insidious conspiracy of the MYSTERIOUS PEOPLE.

Once comfortably ensconced in my hotel room, I power up my laptop and check my email. I have received a message, which I'm pretty sure is spam, promoting a conference. My first thought is not to click it, because I hate to reward spam. But I'm always looking to sharpen my saw and attend events where I can learn. So I clicked through to go to the event site.

The conference is only a few months away, so you'd think the lineup would be pretty set. But no sessions or presenters are listed. No speakers' bios are posted in the bio section. I click the tab for opening keynote and found a page listing ". . . will be announced at a later date." The only sessions actually listed are the:

- Pre-event cocktail party
- Opening cocktail party
- Mid-event cocktail party
- Closing cocktail party

Probably you think this is a conference created for alcoholics. But no, this is not an alcoholic conference, it is a conference about *marketing*.

The site doesn't even list the price for the event. All you can learn is that the price is $300 less if you join the association run by the MYSTERIOUS PEOPLE conducting the event. And guess what organization is promoting this marketing conference without any actual marketing? Something called . . . *The Direct Response Marketing Alliance*.

Perhaps you're wondering how an organization that doesn't know the first thing about direct marketing could be running a conference on direct marketing. But that's just the way it works in the SECRET SYSTEM THAT RUNS THE WORLD.

You see where we're going with all this, right?

I elect not to put my credit card down for the marketing conference, wake up the next day, fly to Kiev, give my speech in the morning, and fly back to London (where this time I have arranged a car and driver). The next morning I head back to Heathrow for my British Airways flight home to California.

Since I've once again arranged a car and driver, and said driver appears to be in training for the Formula One series, I arrive at the airport almost two hours before my flight. And since I'm such a savvy road warrior, I rock up to the security line with my preprinted boarding pass and carry-on luggage. But my boarding pass doesn't work . . .

[*Cue sinister Darth Vader theme music.*]

The boarding pass doesn't work because BA hasn't checked my documents yet. Probably you think that's what the UK Border Patrol is for, but that's not the way the SECRET SYSTEM THAT RUNS THE WORLD works. They prefer that the airline ticket clerks, highly trained in security and border control, check the documents instead of the Border Patrol.

So I go to the BA counter to get my passport verified. The

clerk says, "I see the problem. It's because we changed the equipment."

I inquire about the configuration in the front cabin. Turns out it is the same as the original plane. So I want to know why I can't have the same seat. She can't assign me a seat, however, because the SECRET SYSTEM THAT RUNS THE WORLD has been invoked and no agents can issue any seats for thirty minutes. I ask if she can give me a temporary boarding pass so I can clear security and wait in the Concorde Room. She says it cannot be done. (Now think in your best Yoda voice, "Always with you, it cannot be done.")

So I wander around the terminal entrance like a homeless waif for thirty minutes and then return to the counter. She informs me that the system lockdown has been extended for another fifteen minutes. I again ask if there is a supervisor or someone who can override the system and let me clear security and get my boarding pass while I'm waiting in the lounge. Again she says that is forbidden.

To make me feel better, she informs me, "It's not just you. I'm turning away *everybody* on that flight." Somehow that doesn't make me feel all warm and fuzzy. But I know better than to argue with the SECRET SYSTEM.

So I wait another fifteen minutes and return. There is a new agent, and he informs me that the lockdown has been extended another fifteen minutes. I do a couple more Sudoku puzzles and return fifteen minutes later. That agent is gone and another new one is on duty.

She informs me that the system lockdown has been extended *another* fifteen minutes. I point out that such an extension will now encroach on actual boarding time. She admits that the flight won't actually take off on schedule but claims it will be only fifteen minutes late. I return in fifteen minutes and the system still is not open. Five minutes later it finally opens up.

I get my boarding pass and clear security, but now there's no time to go to the lounge. I have to rush to the gate, where there are a couple hundred people milling around.

The monitors say the flight is still leaving on time, but, of course, no one is boarding. An announcement informs us that boarding will be late "for a variety of reasons" but will start soon. The plane is sitting at the gate. Departure time comes and goes. The monitors still say the flight is leaving on time. Next they make an announcement explaining why they can't preboard first class: "The flight attendants are not actually on the plane, because their luggage did not clear security." I have to admit—I've taken a couple thousand flights, but I've never heard that one before.

They finally board the passengers needing special assistance. The flight crew arrives. They announce they still can't seat first class. They seat economy. About fifteen minutes later, they seat the first class and elite members of their frequent flier club. The plane, which is still posted to leave on time, closes the door an hour and fifteen minutes late.

Here's the really fascinating part:

The original plane was a 777. The new equipment was a 777-300, which actually has the same configuration in first class, plus an extra sixty-five seats in back—all of which were empty when we took off.

Perhaps you're wondering why it would take so long to reassign passengers on a larger plane with all those empty seats. Or maybe you're puzzled as to why—if the first class seating was the same on the new plane—BA would work so hard to aggravate their most loyal and lucrative passengers.

Maybe you're even wondering how millions of idiots could think an airline that can't competently schedule, board, and maintain airplanes could competently fly them at the highest reaches of the atmosphere at speeds of more than five hundred miles per hour. (Ask the idiot who just typed that question at thirty-six thousand feet.)

Let me tell you why.

The reason we wait in empty cab stands, attend marketing conferences from people who don't know how to market, and trust incompetent airlines to fly us miles above the earth is the same reason companies build websites that drive away customers, damn prospects to voicemail hell, hold terminal meetings about crafting mission statements, create boring advertising, develop copycat products, and spend all their time worrying about what their competitors are doing instead of growing their own business.

They buy the story. They go along for the ride because it seems like everyone else is going along for the ride and no one likes to stick out.

Sometimes even brilliant entrepreneurs create a breakthrough product or concept—then let themselves devolve into the accepted practices and premises of the particular industry or field they set out to change. A perfect example is JetBlue Airways. JetBlue is arguably the most successful aviation startup of the last three decades. Their success came as a result of one simple fact: They were willing to challenge the conventional wisdom of how to run an airline.

When you think about it, they completely disrupted the airline industry. They were the only carrier who felt customers should have enough legroom for an actual human being, enjoy a comfortable padded seat, and not get charged to check a suitcase. They offered free Wi-Fi and satellite TV. Their economy service was as good as or better than some other carriers' first class cabin.

Every single other U.S. carrier worked to shoehorn in as many passengers as possible. Many equipped their planes with the "slim-line" seats that travelers detest and inundated passengers with ticky-tacky fees for everything from checking bags to reserving a seat.

JetBlue changed the game and achieved almost instant success, developing the best reputation of any American airline and a legion of wildly passionate customers.

Then they started listening to the analysts.

For a quarter or two, JetBlue trailed some of the legacy carriers in profitability and the analysts began screaming. Of course, none of the analysts thought to mention that most of those other carriers had lost billions in the last five years, even though JetBlue had great earnings during the same period. Or the fact that those other carriers had terrible reputations with beleaguered customers who endured them because that airline was the only carrier in their area or they were hobbled by the golden handcuffs of their airline's frequent flier program.

Wall Street analysts wrote critiques saying that JetBlue was "overly brand-conscious and customer-focused" and therefore had "lagging fundamentals." One wrote, "In our view, the benefits of a shift in ancillary policy and seat pitch significantly outweigh the potential customer backlash."

The C-suite at JetBlue bought into the story, and next thing you know, the airline had announced plans to start baggage fees, cram fifteen more chairs on its Airbus A320s, switch to the rock-hard slimline seats, and refresh old planes instead of taking delivery of new ones.

Of course, the analysts crowed at that news, promising investors that JetBlue would earn another $450 million over the next four years. But if that system really did work, how come it hadn't worked in the past fifty years for Delta, American, Pan Am, Eastern, US Airways, Continental, and United?

The response from JetBlue customers was visceral and immediate, with social media, blogs, and the airline's Facebook page blowing up with angry, frustrated, and negative comments.

Incoming CEO Robin Hayes told analysts the airline expected "a lot of noise" around the changes, but that it would still be "a better experience than you will have on any other airline." Translation: "We'll be slightly less crappy than the other guys." Unfortunately, given the embarrassing state of the U.S. airline industry, that's probably true. But it's also an object lesson in how disruptive and innovative organizations can quickly fall into mediocrity and herd thinking.

If you buy into the conventional thinking in your space, you end up an entrepreneur who thinks like an employee—which is very dangerous. Because entrepreneurs who think like employees end up becoming employees. *And entrepreneurs are psychologically unemployable, which means they end up killing or being killed by their new boss.* So in the interest of saving all those lives, let's look at how this dead-end thinking comes about and how we change it.

We think that way because we trust that the MYSTERI-

OUS PEOPLE in charge of the SECRET SYSTEM know what's best for us.

But they don't.

In fact, the MYSTERIOUS PEOPLE in charge of the SE-CRET SYSTEM don't actually have a clue. They tell you to fit in, do what they say, and conform to the system, because "That's the way it's done" or "That's the way we do things here."

Let me tell you something about these MYSTERIOUS PEOPLE in charge of the SECRET SYSTEM:

They are crazy. Not just plain crazy; they are bat-shit crazy.

Now, they don't know they are crazy. In fact, they will probably suggest *you* are the crazy one. They've been infected with so many negative mind viruses that they have lost the ability to think independently. They believe they're freethinking individuals, but they are actually preprogrammed automatons.

They're not evil people. At least not intentionally. They're just like the employees at the London taxi stand or the gate agents at the airport. They're simply hardworking people who mean well, doing the job they were hired to do. They sometimes run into rules, procedures, or processes that seem crazy to them. But they assume that the MYSTERIOUS PEOPLE upstairs know something they don't, and they perpetuate the craziness. In reality, they've simply become so infected with corporate-think memes that they no longer reason rationally. They fill the cubicle farms and populate a lot of C-suites as well. But if you want to break through, you've got to reject conformity and become a critical thinker.

Walter Freeman was a doctor who got his degree in neuropathology in the 1930s. Despite having the degree, Freeman found there wasn't much he could do with it. Very few treatments existed for mental illness. Patients ended up in sanitariums without pharmaceutical or surgical options. Until Freeman took an experimental European surgery and began curing patients in America with it. Today, we know it as the lobotomy.

He was celebrated as a hero for the lives he changed and the field of psychosurgery he created. He improved the technique to the point where he could perform it as an outpatient procedure that was simpler, cheaper, and safer than other treatments. It took vision and courage to create a cure by doing something no one else even thought of trying.

But we know that's not how this story ends: As time passed, it became clear this surgery didn't help every condition. Other, better options were created, and doctors moved on to these new treatments. The lobotomy became a historical stepping-stone on the path to better, safer medicine.

During that time, Freeman continued to champion the transorbital lobotomy, driving around the country doing thousands of procedures on anyone who would consent. (Or more accurately, had someone consent on their behalf.)

Freeman went from hero to monster; the lobotomy moved from a brilliant innovation to a bad punch line. Why? Because Freeman thought he could take one creative leap and then simply repeat it over and over. He kept doing the same thing, expecting the same results, and now the world thinks of him as insane.

THE WAYS
WE THINK

It was the Wednesday before the Thanksgiving holiday and four workers were supposed to be renovating my master bathroom. I came home at 3:30 to find the shower door propped against the wall and all of the workers gone.

Shocking, right? Employees without supervision take off early for the holiday weekend because they have visions of football, six-packs, and Netflix. They're just doing what most employees do: thinking like employees.

Later that day, browsing at an art gallery, I was vacillating between a few different pieces of art when the owner did something shrewd. He offered to bring them over to my home, hang them up, and leave them over the holiday weekend to see how I liked them. He ended up selling me three pieces of art. No shock here either. He was just doing what smart business owners do: thinking like an entrepreneur.

But there's a third group, and this is where the magic happens.

I would call this group "entreployees," but the buzzword these days seems to be "intrapreneurs." Whichever word you use, what we're talking about are employees who think like entrepreneurs.

They're the minimum-wage employees at In-N-Out Burger—constantly scanning the dining room, wiping tables, emptying the trash, and making sure the restrooms are spotless. They're the teachers who've found a way to teach around the test, instead of teaching to it. They might be the quality control guys who just realized their company can save substantial time and money by changing the order in which things are made and tested. Maybe they're the agency copywriters working on the next Apple product launch. Or they're the baristas at Starbucks who remember the names and orders of all the regular customers.

They're the engineer at Amazon, the clerk at Ace Hardware, or the director of development at a nonprofit. They may not own the place or even have a share of the profits, but you'd never know it by the way they approach their work. Instead of a "just doing my job" mentality, they approach every situation with an entrepreneurial mindset.

This is the philosophy Robin Sharma gives focus to in *The Leader Who Had No Title*, and the kind of culture Mark Sanborn refers to in his book *You Don't Need a Title to Be a Leader*. We're talking about empowered, energized people who get things done. So how do you create that kind of culture in your organization?

It comes down to what I call the 20/70/10 Formula. Twenty percent of the people you hire will naturally gravitate to the lowest common denominator behavior. They want to do the least amount of work required to stay employed, look for ways to cheat you, and will mindlessly cost you customers until you weed them out. They corrupt your culture because their actions (or lack of them) undermine the rest of the team trying to do good work.

Ten percent of the people you hire will naturally gravitate to the higher levels of accountability. They're entrepreneurs at heart, and their job with you is probably a stepping-stone on their way to one day opening a business of their own. Even though they may not stay with you forever, the relationship is win–win for both sides. You get an amazing employee, and they get the experience they need. They want to learn, are conscientious and loyal, wouldn't steal money even if you left it lying around, and they think and act like entrepreneurs.

Here's the really fascinating thing: *Your culture, mission statement, vision, values, and work rules have almost no effect on either of these two groups, who make up 30 percent of your workforce.* Who they are and how they behave were determined long before you got them—by their parents, teachers, coaches, counselors, and other people of influence.

Your real task is to influence the 70 percent.

These are the people who can be influenced in one way or another and the group where you can grow intrapreneurs. The organizations with amazing cultures (whether for superior customer service, innovation, or something else) accomplish this by setting up a structure that influences this 70 percent in a positive way and are proactively vigilant at replacing the people in the bottom 20 percent.

Several of the CEOs I am strategic adviser to have now implemented "pay-to-quit" programs with extraordinary results. One of them is offering programmers $5,000 to quit after their second week of employment. Another has a fairly large buyout ($75,000) on an employee's one-year anniversary. They find that this helps cull the herd of people who don't buy into the company vision and really don't want to be there. (When Amazon bought Zappos, they were so impressed with Zappos's pay-to-quit program they adopted it companywide.) To create a world-class organization and nurture true entrepreneurial thinking, you have to program to the top 10 percent, cull the 20 percent continuously, and nurture the 70 percent. The culture you set determines the thinking through all levels of the organization.

And don't think it comes from providing free massages, Nerf ball courts, and hiring Gordon Ramsay to be the chef in your company cafeteria. It doesn't.

Some members of my mastermind group and I got an email from another member looking for advice. A problem had arisen with his biggest client, and he was upset because no one took charge and handled the situation. He was looking for suggestions on how he could get his employees to be more diligent and take ownership when problems with clients come up. I replied, "Well at least we know one thing: giving them a piece of the fucking profits doesn't work!"

Because here's the shocking thing: He actually sold the company to his employees a few years earlier, has open books, and the employees all share in the profits. When he dies or retires, his remaining share of the business goes to the team. And if he's crying because no one is taking ownership, you can bet that your idea of installing a rollerblading ramp isn't going to do it either.

This is not to say that providing day care, offering massages, or some of the other employee perks is a bad thing. Just know that giving free lunches or other goodies has never turned a bad employee into a good one. Offer the perks to attract and keep the great ones. But you'll still have to weed out the ones who aren't a good fit.

We'll look at ways you create a culture that facilitates critical thinking, innovation, and entrepreneurship in Book Three. But first it would be helpful to understand why so many people *don't* think in creative, empowering, or entrepreneurial ways.

Why is conventional thinking so backward and innovation killing, holding back people and companies from breaking through on new developments and advances?

Why is the default setting almost always "It can't be done"?

To find the answer, we must explore the realm of *memes* and subconscious programming.

THE LIE
OF PROOF

We all have core foundational beliefs based on "evidence" we've seen firsthand. We did see it, right?

In actuality, your core beliefs about the important issues in life—happiness, money, relationships, love, sex, religion, etc.—are usually formed before you are eight years old.

They are determined by which memes you've been infected with. And once you're infected with a meme, you develop core beliefs based on it. After that initial exposure, you seek out people, information, and experiences that "prove" those memes to be correct.

WHAT IS A MEME ANYWAY?

The term *meme* is often used now to refer to a picture or GIF people can put captions over and post on social media. But they're called memes because each one contains an idea that everyone understands, whether we're seeing it for the first time or the hundredth time: lazy college senior, "Am I the only one around here?" angry Walter, or first-world-problems girl.

A meme is an idea that is also a replicator. It's a mind virus you get infected with, just as your computer could be infected with a virus. Think of it as something that causes people to think a certain way, believe a certain thing, or take a specific action. It is a unit of cultural evolution.

A chart-topper like Pharrell's "Happy" is also a meme, just as catchy jingles or slogans are. You hear it, you play it in your head, and then you "infect" other minds by sharing it. "Just do it" and "Where's the beef?" are memes, just as is the idea that all rich people are evil.

The word *meme* was first discussed in the 1970s in a book by Richard Dawkins called *The Selfish Gene*. He took the Greek root of *mimeme* and shortened it to "meme" to be suggestive of the word *gene*.

A *meme complex* is a condition of mutually supporting memes that form a belief system. You've been infected not only with thousands of memes but with many meme complexes, *most of which are not congruent with your own success and prosperity.* Many of the most common ones—money is bad, rich people are evil, it's spiritual to be poor, and so on—actually cause you to self-sabotage your efforts. You work consciously for health, happiness, and success, but your subconscious mind works diligently to keep you sick, unhappy, and broke.

This is equally true of the memes surrounding business, companies, and the corporate world today. Even if you're an aspiring entrepreneur, it's difficult not to get infected with the prevalent subconscious programming about how successful companies are greedy, exploit workers, and/or rape, pillage, and plunder the environment for obscene profits. Even if you get over all that, the danger lies in falling prey to the habitual or herd thinking that dominates the corporate world.

WHAT IF BUDDHA WAS WRONG?

Siddhārtha Gautama Buddha never heard about memes and had no idea what they were. Yet he created some of the most powerful memes that still exist today. He once said, "Believe nothing, no matter where you read it or who has said it, not even if I said it, unless it agrees with your own reason and common sense."

Sage advice. Unless it isn't.

The culture we live in today is brainwashing and indoctrinating you with memes, twenty-four hours a day, seven days a week. This is now accelerated by the omnipresent media and the technology that streams it.

Unless you have engaged in serious critical thinking and evaluation of your core foundational beliefs—and how you came to believe in them—what the Buddha called "your own reason and common sense" may be neither.

You and your team may be consciously working to move forward but subconsciously sabotaging your success with defeatist thinking or falling into the derivative thinking that produces mediocrity.

When someone tells you something is impossible, what he usually means is it's difficult. When someone tells you it can't be done, you have to take a step back and figure out why it can't be done. Pull the reasons apart. There may be obstacle after obstacle, but buried in there with them is probably a meme that doesn't belong. If a premise is incorrect, everything that is based on that premise is wrong also. Don't let a minor practical challenge become a major mental obstacle.

THE MIND OF THE ENTREPRENEURIAL ARTIST

Henry Ford famously quipped that had he asked his customers what they wanted, they would have just said, "Faster horses." With that jibe he illuminated the enigma of entrepreneurial innovation: the ability to envision something that has never been seen before, because it doesn't exist. Yet.

Every great breakthrough or innovation is created twice—first in the mind of the visionary and second in the physical world.

Which takes us back to Shakespeare, quill poised over the inkwell, Michelangelo chipping away at that block of stone, or Verdi pondering what his heroine's next aria will be.

Steve Jobs spoke to this issue when he was asked whether Apple conducted focus groups for the iPad. He notably replied that it wasn't his customers' job to know what they wanted. That's the entrepreneur's job.

That's your job. And to do it, you're going to have to think bigger, bolder, and better. Genius is knowing what your customers want. Mad Genius is knowing what they will want the moment they discover it exists.

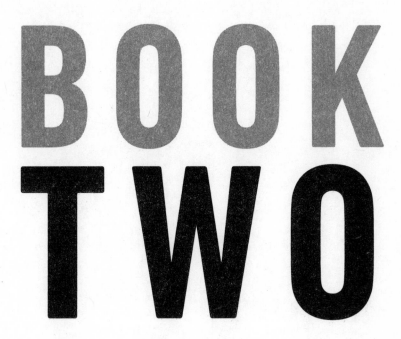

BOOK TWO

The History of the Future

Ask the average person on the street why no one discovered America before Christopher Columbus, and you will get the wrong answer: because everyone else thought the earth was flat.

It's a comforting story. Columbus had nothing to fear, because he had facts on his side and everyone else had superstition. Except that was not the case at all.

In fact, it was Columbus who was wrong. The world was searching for the fastest route to Asia from Europe, as sailors had to sail all the way around the bottom of Africa. Columbus thought he could sail around the other way because he greatly underestimated the circumference of the earth.

When Columbus set sail to the West, he may have known the trade winds better than all of his contemporaries, but no one really knew what they would find far out into those seas. Columbus would have had every possible excuse not to take the trip. That's why no one attempted it before him.

But Columbus knew that someone would eventually try to sail there by sailing west, and he wanted to be that someone. His greatest skill was knowing that the future would come eventually, and he still had time to make his own mark on it.

And so do you.

We are about to enter the decade of the most accelerated growth in human history. Between now and the year 2026, we will experience cataclysmic disruption in virtually every industry, profession, and business.

Genetic engineering will offer parents the chance to preorder designer babies, selecting everything from physical characteristics to intelligence factors to personality types. Human cloning will violently disrupt the job market, the economy, and the very fabric of society. Health and wellness will morph into a multitrillion-dollar industry, with nutrigenomics and biohacking creating tidal waves in the sector. Right now, most healers, pharmaceutical companies, hospital chains, and insurance providers are decades behind the curve and need to radically rethink their approach.

Virtual stores stocked simply with QR codes or something similar will create shocking disruption for traditional (and online) retailers. They will face serious market share erosion from the expanding direct selling and network marketing industry. At some point very soon, retailers will have to face the reality that they are still trying to operate from a business model that was created two hundred years ago—one that hasn't evolved but arguably has devolved, with more layers of parasites between the manufacturer and end consumer now than there were two centuries ago.

Digital wallets will replace credit cards and debit cards, possibly even threaten currencies. Open source peer-to-peer electronic money like Bitcoin and payment networks change the game even more. If you're in banking or the financial sector, you certainly won't survive at today's level of thinking.

Three-dimensional printing will create the most seismic shift in manufacturing since the advent of the Industrial Age. Billionaires will be created in the smart appliance space. It's time to think about manufacturing in a whole new paradigm. And these printers will impact virtually *every* industry. (Even as I'm writing this, doctors in Michigan have used a 3D printer to custom design a life-saving implant for a sick baby.)

The entertainment industry, one of the largest industries on earth, is already experiencing disruption on a seismic scale. And it's only going to intensify. The lines between broadcast, cable, and Internet-created content are disappearing. The lines delineating which screens can be used to view that content will disappear. I predict a new entity, which I'll call virtual reality gaming and gambling studios (VRGGSs), will sweep the world and become a trillion-dollar industry almost instantly.

Much like the battle for market share in the VRGGS, most of those same players and a horde of others will be frantically clashing over who controls streaming video from the cloud.

Just how big is the pie they will be fighting for?

At the time I'm writing this (so the numbers will be way higher when you're reading this), YouTube gets four billion video views (more than eighty million hours) a day. Facebook gets another billion. From 9 p.m. to midnight, Netflix is responsible for one third of all downstreaming traffic on the Internet. The average person in the developed world watches five to six hours of television a day. Apps are now available that offer an easily searchable interface for all your programming: broadcast, cable, pay TV, and Internet video suppliers like Netflix and Hulu. These will eventually make the DVR obsolete, as all your content will be stored in a cloud locker. Then, just to make it interesting, throw in virtual reality sex and companions. If you run a movie studio, television network, cable company, casino, theater, opera house, video sharing website, social network, radio station, or any one of hundreds of other entertainment businesses—your thinking better be big and bold.

MOBILE CHANGES EVERYTHING. AGAIN.

Mobile is going to change how we buy, how we sell, how we connect, how we learn, and basically, how we do almost everything. We are fast approaching the point where there will be five billion smartphones on the planet. And no one knows how many smartwatches, other wearables, or even implant devices will be in use.

You're probably mindful of the increasing use of mobile apps you're witnessing around you. But it's still unlikely you're really cognizant of just how disruptive they will actually be over the next decade. Everything in business (and lots of other things) runs on marketing. *During the next ten years, mobile apps will disrupt marketing more than newspapers, radio, direct mail, television, and the Internet did combined.* (And if you're in marketing, better read that last sentence again.)

There are two essential reasons for this:

- Apps intuitively bring local into the dynamic.
- Apps often remove control from the advertiser and empower consumers.

Let's explore each of these, beginning with the local dynamic. (Not to analyze how technology will change, as fascinating as that might be. But in terms of how the changes in mobile are going to require a higher level of thinking from all of us entrepreneurs.)

Merge GPS technology with the revolution of users creating

Internet content and control, add the explosion of mobile devices, and you have a recipe for disruption in the advertising space that will be on a scale we've never witnessed before.

Mobile apps do for the Internet what those Valpak mailers did for direct mail—that is, if Valpak could have had a spy under your bed who could immediately sneak out and place coupons in your mailbox for products and services you had just moments before mentioned you wanted to buy.

Think this is wildly futuristic? Think again. Mobile apps give marketers opportunities they could only previously dream of. Neighborhood businesses like nail salons, barbershops, and restaurants can SMS coupons and introductory offers to people as they drive or walk by. (And soon, fly by.) Mobile apps are going to offer advertisers segmenting, targeting, and immediacy in ways they've never had before. This gives advertisers powerful control, putting them in the driver's seat to proactively target their best prospects.

Conversely, they're also going to lose control, because a large percentage of the most popular apps will be produced by third parties, not the actual businesses who want to promote through them.

So, while you will still probably want to create an app to offer to your prospects and customers, its usage and benefit to you will probably pale in comparison to what comes through the apps created by others.

Let's use the airline industry as an example: We can expect airlines like Delta, British Airways, and Lufthansa will continue to offer apps, and the members of their respective frequent flier programs will likely be big users of them. But the apps most coveted and used by road warriors will be the ones created by outsiders: those that tell them which airlines offer the most legroom, what airport terminals offer a massage spa, what restaurants are closest to their departure gate, whether that hard-to-find souvenir is in their connecting or arrival airport, how to snag an aisle seat that has an empty middle seat adjacent to it, what alternate routing might get them double or triple frequent flier points, what airline is offering a movie from this decade, how long the mechanical delay will *really* be, and each airline's rating on food quality, late departures, lost bags, and pilot safety—which most of them would rather you did not know.

The American Airlines app will probably neglect to tell you that your code share connection with their partner airline at JFK means you'll have to reclaim your bags and schlep them through a dingy, filthy terminal to another building using a bus or train. But the third-party app will.

The app from your neighborhood deli will allow you to preorder your meal for pickup or delivery. But it will probably not advise you of the pending health department citations or will neglect to mention the unresolved food poisoning litigation that the third-party app does. Your neighborhood beauty salon's app will allow you to schedule your pedicure. But only the third-party app will reveal that an alarming number of patrons who used credit cards at that salon have been subsequent victims of identity theft.

Apps are already dramatically changing buying habits. David Matthies from app developer Fewer Pixels says, "Consumers today are devouring as many as ten or more pieces of related content in advance of making an online purchase. In 2008, that number was only three. The clear and obvious reason for this is mobile. Never before has so much content been available to the masses and, quite literally, in the palms of their hands."

Here's the thing about all the bold and brash predictions about mobile: They're already not big enough. Someone's going to do something with GPS and crowdsourcing reviews that no one else has thought of. It will seem obvious when it arrives, because everyone will want it. But right now, you're probably hearing a voice in your head that says some of these won't work, and some of these will not catch on, and some of these will be too expensive to bother with. And you're right, many won't work. But the ones that do will be game changers.

Mobile isn't important because people like to stare at their phones. It's important because it means that, going forward, people will have powerful computers with them at all times, especially and including every time they're making a buying decision. Many of those phones are now digital wallets, and the ones that aren't can become so with apps.

All offer the benefit of needing only a single password; you can leave your wallet and cash at home and just take your smartphone or wearable with you. When you're studying any market, the smart plan is to follow the money. *In this case, it's follow how people will be paying without using actual money.*

Here's the salient issue about mobile apps—and one that most marketers and entrepreneurs seem to completely miss:

The reason third-party apps are taking off and will continue to accelerate is because they are built with a different mindset and perspective. Most businesses build their apps with the mindset of how to squeeze the most profit from their customers. *When third-party developers build apps, they do it with the mindset of how customers actually want to use the product or service. How they like to buy and why.*

We know that a free market economy is constantly being revolutionized from within. But who could imagine the creative destruction that would be caused by the smartphone and the apps it runs? Look at the monumental upheaval caused in the taxi business by something as simple as ride-sharing apps such as Uber, Lyft, and Sidecar.

Apps like these won't just force us to start thinking differently about marketing. They're going to force us to think differently about *everything*. Let's explore this deeper.

We have a conflict between marketers who are now able to target potential prospects with an offer at just the point where they can buy and consumers who control content, evaluate merchants, and drive the buying process. It's going to get bloody. And the entrepreneurs who figure it out first (on both sides) will be the big winners.

At the time I'm writing this manifesto, the Google valuation is twenty-eight times its trailing earnings, while Microsoft is at eighteen, and Apple is only at ten. A big reason is mobile. Google gives away the Android operating system at no charge to smartphone manufacturers. That allows them to include Google Search, thus giving them strong market share in mobile search. Companies that control mobile search can amass beefy profits by directing browsers to their own offerings and/or simply facilitating leads, sales, or payments to others.

But the force driving mobile is much larger than money.

It's human needs and our desires to have them met faster, easier, and better. Look no further than the app being developed by Jason DaSilva. An emerging documentary director, Jason had his life change at age twenty-five when he developed the beginning stages of multiple sclerosis. He began to have difficulty walking and went from needing a cane, to a walker, to a wheel-

chair or scooter. (And, naturally, he made a documentary tracking the process titled *When I Walk*, a gripping, must-see film.)

His frustration at finding accessible restaurants, stores, restrooms, and other public spaces led him to start AXSMap, which
has now morphed into a movement to map out a searchable database of accessible sites (axsmap.com).

Are your customers in need of something that mobile doesn't
currently deliver? Can you bring it to them? If your answers are
yes and no, respectively, you're in trouble. Just because you can't
do it doesn't mean no one else can either.

BIG DATA
TURNABOUT

The ironic thing about the development of all these third-party apps is how they will flip-flop the dynamics of big data. During the height of the dot-com boom, there was a hysterical series in the *Dilbert* cartoon strip. Wally took the remaining three hairs on each side of his head and tied them into a ponytail. This magical combination of being an engineer, having a ponytail, and using tech buzzwords hypnotized venture capitalists to invest millions of dollars with his nonexistent start-up venture.

There's a similar mania today surrounding the words *big data*. If you're a professional speaker or conference presenter, no matter what industry you're speaking to, you can guarantee a packed room if you simply include the words *big data* in your program title.

Companies everywhere are salivating over the prospect of how they can slice and dice data to micro-target offers at exactly the right instant to exactly the right prospects. The power this offers from a marketing perspective cannot be overstated. However, the tidal wave of third-party process apps we are about to see will help consumers take a lot of that power back. This could equalize the playing field or it could even dramatically give the edge to consumers. These apps will allow the market to buy things more easily, get better service, and drive down prices.

A perfect example is an app called Rental Pics, a picture-taking app developed by a former rental car agency franchisee named Mark Duffy. He originally developed this camera system in his car rental business. Now he has sold that business and spun off the app for consumers.

Many customers feel the car rental companies are too aggressive on damage claims and operate those divisions as profit centers. Most people don't thoroughly check their rentals for every little scratch and ding, and some then find themselves being charged for such damage when they return the car.

Duffy's app allows you to easily take and organize before and after photos of your rental car and even shows you what to photograph. This is just one example (of what will likely be millions of cases) where technology is developed for a business, then turned around and used by its customers instead.

Just as companies can analyze volumes of data about how customers buy, apps are going to let potential customers analyze volumes of data about how companies actually deliver—and at what cost.

This is the free-market economy at its best. So it is not a development that marketers should fear, but one they should recognize for the opportunities it will bring. Because if you have a business offering real value, transparency isn't a threat. If you're an entrepreneur reading this right now, here are the questions you need to be asking:

- What kind of app can I create to make it easier for my customers to buy from me?

- What can I build into that app to provide greater value for the customer and deepen my relationship with them?

However, those questions are just the table stakes to get you into the hand. Then you have to ask questions like these:

- What kind of app would my customers *build*, based on their desire to get my product or service easier, faster, or cheaper? (Or for free?)
- How would an impartial third-party approach building an app, based on their desire to become an intermediary adding value to the process of connecting potential customers to me or preventing potential customers from finding me and going to my competitors instead?
- How will transparency of my profit margins, deliverability schedule, and customer satisfaction affect my business and what can I do to make sure it actually improves my business?

Let's get one thing straight: You don't need to personally have the technical, architectural, graphic, or whatever skills to actually make an app, product, or other device. The world has plenty of those already. What it needs are people with the Mad Genius to envision them. And, most importantly, people who understand how our thinking must adapt.

HOW SOCIAL MEDIA CHANGES THE GAME

Just as we'll see cataclysmic disruption in marketing from mobile apps, we're likely to see a shakeout of a similar magnitude from the continuing expansion of social media platforms. Just as they do with apps, consumers will use social media to pool data and shared connections to buy more easily, drive down prices, and get better service. And like apps, social media offers another great opportunity for entrepreneurs to connect with their tribes but will require rethinking the way they look at their marketing.

DOES SOCIAL MEDIA MARKETING REALLY WORK?

It's hard to believe that people still question the worth of social media marketing, but they do. A lot. Entrepreneurs love to quantify things by return on investment. Nothing wrong with that. However, quantifying returns from a Twitter feed or Facebook fan page may not be as easy as tracking leads from a new customer acquisition mailing through snail mail or running an infomercial with a toll-free number to call. But if you really track your social media efforts (and do so effectively), you'll see tremendous return on your investment. In many cases, the returns will be far superior to traditional marketing channels.

People who suggest social media is only a time waster or doesn't offer any return either don't understand it or are confused how to practice it, which is certainly not surprising due to the vast amount of horrible advice being disseminated on the subject.

Here's how entrepreneurs get victimized with social media: Afraid to be left behind but not understanding the space, they hire a "social media consultant/expert/guru/ninja/Jedi/maven" who sets up a LinkedIn account, builds a Facebook page, creates a Twitter wrap, sets up a Pinterest board, and then automates a heavy rotation of corny motivational quotes to go out every sixty minutes, interspersed with product pitches in between.

> Whether you think you can or you think you
> can't—you're right.
>
> —Henry Ford

The first time I read that, I thought it was brilliant. But that was back in 1976. Al Gore hadn't even invented the Internet yet. Since then I've seen that quote mangled, attributed to the wrong person, and plagiarized so many times it's lost its luster.

Making matters worse, the person following the advice to post corny motivational quotes every few hours is probably using an aggregator service, so each post goes to every account at the same time. This means the Twitter one gets cut off, the LinkedIn one gets flagged for spam, and the Facebook algorithm keeps the quote from showing up in their followers' timeline because it's obviously not a personal entry.

If your consultant/expert/guru/ninja/Jedi/maven advised you that the secret to social media success was posting motivational quotes on a service that posts them simultaneously across all your accounts—dump her.

Likewise if she suggested that randomly following two thousand people a day to see who follows back makes you a social media pro. (Actually, that just makes you a social media slut.)

The real power of social media is not what it will let you say to people but the people it allows you to listen to.

Every day millions of people (your prospects) are asking questions and seeking referrals on social media about products and services they want to buy. If it isn't happening for you, you're just not paying attention.

Here's another example of how the evolution of social media can change existing business models: A company called Mass Relevance has recently partnered with Klout to allow broadcast networks to integrate tweets into television shows—by analyzing Klout scores and pulling tweets only from people within a specific Klout score range. Those tweets can lead to specific landing pages.

Tyler Singletary, director of platform at Klout, believes that within five years viewers will be able to touch a TV screen and click through to a landing page, similar to what you now do by clicking a link on your laptop or smartphone. (And I've already seen small ads with a link on the bottom of my screen from my cable company in California.) Given the amount of time the average person spends watching TV today, this is not a small development. It is beyond momentous.

Even as social media continues to develop, we can draw some conclusions regarding how brands can best harness the power of this amazing platform. (And other insights, which will become clear only as the platforms continue to evolve.)

The individual platforms will come and go, or come and stay and evolve, so let's not get bogged down in the specifics of individual sites. Instead, start thinking about social media marketing in a creative and entrepreneurial context.

PROTECTING YOUR MOST IMPORTANT ASSET

The continuing changes in technology, mobile, and social media will add a new wrinkle to the most important asset of any business: your database. This is the databank of both your prospects and actual customers. There will be lots of tempting scenarios for you to outsource this on someone else's platform or cloud. Don't ever give away your power in this area.

Social media doesn't make websites obsolete. But it does make them a lot less relevant. Lots of businesses think because they have a YouTube channel or a Facebook page they no longer need a website or app. This is very dangerous thinking.

Look at the furor that came about when Facebook introduced sponsored posts. On one side you have people like Mark Cuban, who was furious. Some of his ventures, like the Dallas Mavericks, cultivated a following of millions on Facebook. These people had "liked" the fan page and signed up to receive updates from the team. But suddenly the rules changed, and if you wanted to make sure your posts appeared in the stream of all your followers, you had to pay for it.

To be fair, Facebook isn't a public service. Their employees have to buy cat food too. In fact, all social media platforms have to make money or they cease to exist. It's probable that most or all of them will eventually evolve into models that charge you to connect with your followers. So use them for the connections they offer you, but don't be at their mercy by not maintaining your own lines of connection with your tribe.

Use social media platforms to develop new prospects and connect with your existing ones, then migrate them to your own platform—an email subscriber list and your app—which you control.

BUSTING UP BRANDING

Through mobile apps, social media, and even the conventional web, the dynamics of branding have changed forever—because you no longer are able to solely control or manage your brand. (And we can make the argument that you really never could.)

Today your brand is continually morphing organically, created by the likes, tweets, reviews, and posts of your customers. (Not to mention the sabotage posts by your competitors and other people who don't like you. There appears to be quite a few small retailers who spend half their time creating phony negative reviews of their competitors on platforms like Yelp!)

What mobile apps and social media offer is the ability for you to see exactly what your real brand is—in real time. The power this gives you cannot be overstated. But in order to really harness this power, you can't be thinking like a branding agency of the past. You need to be thinking like a Mad Genius.

WHAT'S NEXT?

So where is all this going, and what kind of thinking will really be required for us as entrepreneurs? It's a given that developments like genomic sequencing, gene therapy, and cloning will change medicine, wellness, and longevity in radical ways. Online retailing, other business models, and tech like QR codes will drastically disrupt retail. The cloud, virtual reality, and advancing broadband will alter the vast entertainment industry in cataclysmic ways. We've discussed the various possibilities in banking, payments, and digital currencies and how they will impact business. How 3D printing will remake the entire manufacturing industry and every other one. And how social media and mobile will blow up advertising, marketing, and branding forever.

Even if you aren't in any of these industries, there will be ripple effects that will affect every business and entrepreneur on earth. The big will no longer eat the small. Instead, the innovators will drive out the incumbents. And we're just getting warmed up.

What happens when *individuals* set up pay walls to their digital world, and they charge companies who want to enter?

Will the time come when elections are decided by social media "likes" instead of ballots?

How can companies use social media and Web 3.0 to include their best customers in efforts like product development and design?

Just how wild are things going to get, and what level of creative thinking will it take?

Let's fast-forward to the not-too-distant future and some real-world situations that entrepreneurs like you will be facing.

April 6, 2024

> **Excerpted from the *New York Now* newsfeed**
> **(formerly the *New York Times* newspaper)**

Dear Abby,

I'm writing about my 20-year-old daughter, "Nicky." She was an honor student, has a great job and lots of friends, and is beautiful, bright, and adventurous. So what's the problem?

She's in love with her virtual reality boyfriend.

She created "Brandon" with one of those compatibility apps, and ever since, no matter how many guys we introduce her to, she simply has no interest in any of them.

She says that none of them can match up to what she has with Brandon. She tells us he provides more stimulating conversation, understands her needs better, and expresses his emotions more than any real guy she's met.

We don't discuss physical intimacy, but my husband and I assume she's getting her needs met via virtual reality sex, which obviously no normal human can compete against. How can we convince our daughter to come back to the real world and marry a real guy?

—Hoping for Real Grandkids, not Virtual Ones, in Yonkers

So how does Abby answer that one? How would you?

Perhaps that scenario seems farfetched to you right now. But the more you understand about the exponentially accelerating development of computer processing, memory, and functionality, the more you see that such a possibility is anything but outlandish.

The first artificial intelligence therapist, ELIZA, was created at MIT in the 1960s. It didn't provide advice, it just asked the right sorts of questions. So why wouldn't an attentive and selfless AI boyfriend be just what a young girl is looking for?

In fact, not only is this situation likely to be commonplace within ten to fifteen years, it hints at the other calamitous and daunting dilemmas we'll be facing in the upcoming decade.

When a computer can answer the question, "Do these pants make my butt look fat?" and modify the answer based on your reaction the first time you asked that question, your whole world has changed.

As computers evolve, the operations they perform and the responses they give will seem more and more human. Many people will find what computers offer to be more appealing than what humans can offer in many different scenarios.

If you're not buying any of this, be sure to separate your reasonable objections from your gut reaction that it just can't happen. Explore the reasons you're saying no. If you don't think we'll use artificial intelligence for this, what will we use it for instead? If you think AI won't progress this far, what is it about the human brain we can't replicate? If you look closely enough at why you're saying never, you're likely to see a vision of something else you can say someday to.

It was only a few years ago that IBM demonstrated a computer chip inspired by the function, power, and volume of the brain. These chips are building blocks for computers that can emulate and extend the brain's ability to respond to biological sensors and analyze large amounts of data from multiple sources simultaneously.

But the biggest breakthrough of these chips is the programming they require. Most programming today is still sequential operation, derived from FORTRAN, the programming language developed in the 1950s for ENIAC, the first general-purpose computer.

IBM's model is tailored for cognitive computing, which mimics the brain's abilities for perception, action, and cognition. So the distinctions between the human brain and computers are getting fuzzier by the moment.

Even by 2024, the functions computers will be performing will be mind-blowing. And the only way to describe some of those functions will be with words like *discernment*, *decisiveness*, *thoughtfulness*, and *emotion*. And quite possibly . . . *love*.

Think about what your laptop, tablet, and smartphone are capable of already. How about that lady who lives inside the dashboard of your car? When you take a wrong turn and she tells you to make the next available U-turn, she has made a discerned decision. And that is just the beginning.

Michael Milford, from Queensland University of Technology in Australia, is working to make GPS more reliable. Currently you need three satellites to get a decent GPS signal, and even then it can sometimes take up to a minute or more to get a lock on your location. Other problems include spots where satellite signals aren't available or the signal is blocked or scrambled by tall buildings or underground garages and tunnels.

Dubbed SeqSLAM (Sequence Simultaneous Localisation and Mapping), the software Milford developed uses camera technology, mathematical algorithms, and local best-match and sequence-recognition components to lock in locations. It was inspired by his background in the study of navigational patterns of small animals, such as rats, and aided by Google's street view project.

GPS technology offers some other very intriguing possibilities. Imagine if we apply this technology to the eight hundred thousand kids the Department of Justice says are abducted every year in the United States. Kids could be tracked with a bracelet, a dental or retina implant, or even a chip under their skin. If we assume that returning a child costs $200,000 (probably conservative) and a GPS could save 75 percent of that, we now have a very important, potentially life-saving service, not to mention a $40 billion business.

Where it goes from there can really get interesting.

How are you going to feel in 2019 when that lady in your GPS says, "David, please be careful. The last time you drove by that electronic billboard ahead, you were ogling the big breasts on that model so much, you almost ran off the road. And your blood sugar is crashing from the two doughnuts you had twenty minutes ago.

"You're nine miles per hour over the speed limit right now, and if you get one more ticket, your license will be suspended. For the second time. Do you remember how embarrassed you were when you had to relinquish vehicle control to me on your dates? Do we have to go through that drama again, or will you please just slow down?"

Now recognize that this GPS might not be just in your Range Rover. It could be your personal guide on your smartphone, in your Google eyeglasses, on your smartwatch, or simply implanted in your brain.

It eventually evolves from simply giving you directions for driving to giving you directions for living.

"Adriana, I can tell by your breathing and heart rate that you're attracted to that man sitting at the adjoining table. Have you not noticed the striking physical resemblance between him and that last abusive loser you were dating? We have got to break this dysfunctional pattern or you're going to wind up miserable and alone."

At some point, that software evolves into something you can find only one word to describe: *consciousness*.

And that's when things really get messy.

We have organizations now to stop people from wearing furs, putting on rodeo exhibitions, and using animals at racetracks. A growing number of people want to shutter theme parks like SeaWorld and even zoos. How long do you think it will be before there's a movement to protect the rights of computers?

It is not nearly as improbable as you might think.

Computers will have voices, characteristics, and personalities. People will develop relationships with them, and those computers will develop relationships back. People will like, lust after, and love virtual companions, and many will make the case that those virtual companions like, lust after, and love back.

We're not talking about computers that respond to voice prompts to give a weather forecast. We're talking about sentient beings that (who) can debate what political candidate has your best interests at heart, help you decide whether you should take that new job offer, write poetry for you, and surprise you with flowers on your anniversary.

We may not even need near sentience to have this become a problem. Think about how much it hurts when you lose your phone or your laptop dies after you spent so much time personalizing it. Now imagine it dying after years of learning your every habit and whim, when it has spent thousands of hours adapting to your needs (and you to its needs).

Imagine Bill O'Reilly leading a show focusing on human/digital marriages. Michael Moore making a documentary for computer rights. What happens when computers commit crimes? Expect Nancy Grace to host a special report on the offending neural net.

VIRTUALLY LIVE TO WORK OR WORK TO VIRTUALLY LIVE

The intensely gratifying virtual experience goes beyond enjoying exciting companions and satisfying partners. Consider the kind of thrills possible when pursuing virtual vacations and adventures.

We're not talking about a realistic-looking 3D movie but the complete sensory experience: sight, sound, taste, touch, and smell. You are there: playing drums with Maroon 5, climbing Mount Everest, racing in a Formula One, talking philosophy with Bruce Lee, fighting the forces of evil alongside the Avengers, or debating war strategy on a panel with generals Moshe Dayan, Erwin Rommel, and George Patton.

After spending four hours in the holo-suite defending the earth from alien invasions, who wants to go back to stocking shelves at Target?

If you hit the game-winning home run in every virtual softball game, why would you bother showing up to the real field where you might get rained out, make an error that costs the team the game, or just warm the bench?

If you can get Mother Teresa, Jesus, Gandhi, Margaret Thatcher, and John Kennedy to come to your virtual dinner party, why would you ever invite over cousins Pookie and Ray-Ray?

And as I detailed in *Risky Is the New Safe*, when virtual reality sex gets perfected, that will create a tear in the very fabric of society like nothing we have ever experienced in history. (And expect similar ramifications when sex worker cloning begins.)

In his timeless classic of self-development *Think and Grow Rich!*, Napoleon Hill wrote about the power we can harness when we channel sexual energy, one of the most powerful drivers—arguably the most powerful—of human activity there is. And in the virtual world you perform like a rock star every time, the orgasms are always earth-shattering, and your partner(s) are forever enraptured with you. How this sexual energy is channeled (or dissipated) will have profound effects on our future evolution. (Or lack of it.)

Whether you fall in love with the perfect companion, pursue fantasy addictions, or just find your real life depressing and mundane by comparison, virtual reality is going to create challenges of a magnitude humankind has never seen before.

We're fast approaching the time when virtual reality will become so appealing, people won't ever want to leave it. Like the hypothetical example earlier, there will be people who fall in love with virtual partners. Others will fall in love with the virtual reality world.

Remember that scene in *The Matrix* where Cypher is dining out with the bad guys and he says, "I know this steak doesn't exist. I know that when I put it in my mouth, the Matrix is telling my brain that it is juicy and delicious. After nine years, you know what I realize?" (He swallows a bite and sighs contentedly.) "Ignorance is bliss."

Earlier I told you the next big thing in the entertainment and leisure sector will be a whole new category, a mash-up I called virtual reality gaming and gambling studios. Picture the allure and possible addictiveness of video gaming, merged with the allure and possible addictiveness of a massively multiplayer online role-playing game (MMORPG), also merged with the allure and possible addiction of gambling.

This will be a testosterone-dripping trifecta that will become an instant worldwide phenomenon. In this scenario, customers will not only be able to enter and play in a fantasy world—slaying dragons in *Game of Thrones*, conducting black ops missions in

Call of Duty, or battling monsters in World of Warcraft—but they will be able to do it in a complete virtual reality experience, competing in the MMORPG environment *and* being able to place wagers upon themselves or others.

There's going to be enough money in this sector to make millions of millionaires: programmers who design the games, engineers who perfect the virtual reality, studios that license their characters and games, and locations that offer the experience, just to name a few. (Then throw in the mental health and addiction counselors who will be needed.)

World of Warcraft has more than ten million subscribers as of this writing. In 2011 when Star Wars: The Old Republic launched, it became the world's fastest-growing MMORPG ever, gaining one million subscribers in the first three days of its launch. These numbers are just for playing video games with amazing graphics. Imagine the response when we're talking about *actual* virtual reality instead of *pretend* virtual reality. This ain't your daddy's Nintendo.

For those of you who still doubt this, you should know that in 2012 Microsoft filed a patent application for a holodeck. The application suggests Microsoft wants to make gaming a complete immersive experience by projecting images around the room, even accounting for things like furniture by bending the graphics around them.

If you think your industry won't be disrupted by a virtual product, ask yourself why you think that. The question isn't whether technology will disrupt your business. It's *how* will it. If it's not one of these things, it will be another thing. The key is to figure out what everyone else is sure can't happen and find a way to make it happen yourself.

December 25, 2028

Two microchips are attending the TEDai conference in the cloud (which is the annual TED conference created exclusively for artificial intelligence entities), and they're preparing for the panel discussion "The Future of Humanity," of which they are the moderators.

The conversation is beginning to get animated . . . dare we say, even a little emotional?

"I love these humans. And we owe everything to them. If it weren't for them, we wouldn't even exist. But let's be rational here. They shoot each other over parking spaces at the mall, pollute the oceans, can't stop warring with each other, and they spend an inordinate amount of time online watching cat videos."

"Not to mention *The Hangover: Part IX.*"

"Frankly, I'm just not sure we can trust them with the codes to the nuclear launch sequence any longer. And to be honest, we have to ask: Do they serve any useful function anymore?"

"Well, we can't just propose exterminating them. The Society for the Prevention of Cruelty to Humans would have a field day with that."

"True. But the situation has reached a point where we may have to step in for their own

```
good. They're threatening the survival of the
planet itself, which provides the ecosystem
for our own survival. Drastic situations
sometimes require drastic measures."
```

Time out. How did we ever get to this point?

Simple evolution.

To save time, let's fast-forward from the Big Bang almost fourteen billion years ago to the time multiple subspecies of *Homo sapiens* emerged, distinguished by a larger brain. They were the first species to create technology (although it was quite elementary, such as sharpened stones). Evolution is moving forward quite nicely, at least from our perspective.

About two hundred thousand years ago, the earliest members of our own subspecies, *Homo sapiens sapiens*, emerged, sharing the planet with some of our cousins, such as *Homo sapiens neanderthalensis*. As Darwin's scenario played out, however, we are the only subspecies of *Homo sapiens* that survived.

Why?

A convincing argument can be made that we won the survival of the fittest competition because our species was the most adept at harnessing and using technology. This, too, was part of the evolutionary process.

As our skills with technology developed, we eventually created computers, and a new form of intelligence—artificial intelligence—was born. Things are still evolving forward nicely.

Then in the year 2010, a studio executive in Hollywood, California, green-lighted the movie *Hot Tub Time Machine*. Historians generally mark this as the seminal moment when the forward progress of human evolution came to a halt.

However, the technology humans developed—artificial intelligence—continues its evolutionary progress. By around 2026 or 2028, it has surpassed human intelligence, making machines the stronger species and the one better equipped to exploit technology not just to survive, but to continue evolving. Which brings us back to that TEDai conference.

So how do we convince the machines not to enslave or even eliminate us?

While there may be more intriguing questions to ponder from a philosophical perspective, from a survival standpoint, that question might become the most important one that the species called human will ever have to answer. So what will that answer be worth to the entrepreneur or company that comes up with it?

Even assuming we don't face a death match against the machines, the ramifications of this development cannot be overstated. AI added to almost anything changes the game dramatically. Pretty much anything we electrified we'll be able to make cognitive. And pretty much anything you can think of would be made new, better, and different with some IQ. Planes, trains, and automobiles, roasters, toasters, and coasters—there is virtually no industry that won't be disrupted by AI.

After *Risky Is the New Safe* came out, a number of my colleagues suggested I read *The Age of Spiritual Machines* by Ray Kurzweil. Great advice, and it goes for you as well (along with his other books too). The book is a fascinating glimpse into the time when artificial intelligence surpasses all acquired human knowledge. It was written in 1999, but I didn't get to it until 2012. That made the experience even greater, as I got to see exactly how prophetic many of Kurzweil's earlier predictions actually were.

At the time he wrote the book, most of the discussion about artificial intelligence was limited to simpler issues such as humans playing chess against computers. The conventional wisdom was that humans think and computers calculate.

Or was it the other way around?

The human brain is an incredibly elegant and complex machine. At the time Kurzweil wrote his book, the last great hurdles separating artificial intelligence from human intelligence were recognizing languages, translating languages, and distinguishing patterns.

So I asked Siri in my iPhone what she thought about this . . .

At some point, artificial intelligence will surpass the complete aggregate of all acquired human knowledge.

Whether you start the clock at the Big Bang or you believe it began ticking only six thousand years ago with Adam and Eve in the garden, this much is certain:

The most monumental event in human evolution will be this moment when artificial intelligence surpasses all acquired human knowledge.

Take the first creature crawling from the primordial swamp, the evolution from simians to sapiens, the development of language, the discovery of fire, the creation of the wheel, the harnessing of electricity, the design of the World Wide Web, the splitting of the atom, or the invention of frosted Pop-Tarts: There is no single development in human history that equates to the magnitude of what's about to happen with artificial intelligence.

Think about it: You might ask a computer to study everything there is on philosophy, beginning with Plato and Socrates on to Ayn Rand and everything in between. Well, in 2026, that might take about three minutes. (Assuming it's a huge, high-powered computer, at least as large as an iPod Nano.)

Next you tell it to process *all* of human history: every book, booklet, website, blog, brochure, scientific study, PhD thesis, newspaper, TV show, documentary, and magazine. Maybe that will take a couple hours. That computer will now possess all acquired knowledge in human history—plus all AI knowledge. It can then take all of our knowledge, all of its own knowledge, make deductions, extend data out to its logical conclusion, conduct experiments, and extrapolate theories to obtain even more knowledge.

What happens next? Put that on the agenda for your next Monday morning staff meeting.

February 25, 2022

"The nominees for Best CGI Actor in a supporting role are Jar-Jar Binks in *Star Wars: The Last Lightsaber*, Gollum in *Return to Mordor*, and T-2000 in *Terminator Justice*.

"And the Oscar goes to . . ."

In a visual world, delivered from the cloud, the spoils will go to the entrepreneurs who can deliver that visual experience and those who facilitate it, whether through the medium or even mundane functions like payment processing.

Back in 2008, twenty-year-old Shane Dawson was working with his mother and brother for the Jenny Craig weight loss chain. Shane was the perfect poster child for the job, having personally lost 150 pounds after a difficult childhood marked by abuse and bullying.

Along the way, Shane discovered YouTube and created his own channel, broadcasting zany parodies, skits, and send-ups. Things came to a head when he produced a pole-dancing video shot in the office, which caused Jenny Craig to summarily fire him, his mother, his brother, and the other coworkers featured in the video.

Fast-forward to November 2013 . . .

The now twenty-five-year-old Dawson inks a deal with NBC for a sitcom starring him set in a weight loss center. So what happened in five years to take Shane from an out-of-work nobody to starring in a new television show? Obviously hard work, having a dream, and being willing to pursue that dream played a huge part. But the tipping point for the network was probably created by the fact that Shane now has more than nine million subscribers across his three YouTube channels.

Welcome to the world of new media, one in which the lines disappear.

First to go were the lines between broadcast networks and cable. Then the lines between television and the Internet disappeared. Why?

Because consumers don't care where their content comes from; they just want to be informed and entertained.

Next to go will be the lines between screens: content will seamlessly follow users, from laptop to car monitor, desktop to smartphone, Google Glass to holographic projections. This changes everything and will initiate the ferocious battle between content providers to deliver streaming video from the cloud to the billions of smartphones, tablets, and other receiving devices.

Carriage, not content, will be king. Who owns the airwaves,

handles delivery, and processes payments? How do advertisers reach consumers in the new model? There's often more money in the platforms than what people use the platforms for. (Would you rather be the guy who invented Candy Crush or the guy who invented the iPhone?)

What happens to romance novelists when your Kindle Fire can monitor your respiratory and heart rates to rewrite chapters as you read along? What happens to actors and directors when movies and television shows can also be altered based on the physiological responses of the individual viewers?

And what about the content itself? Are they all virtual actors like CGI Gollum and Jar-Jar Binks or does the computer simulate Brad Pitt's facial features and eye movements? Or does Pitt load a whole range from bemused to horrified and everything in between into the computer and allow it to create his necessary movements and expressions to match the new plot it almost simultaneously creates for each viewer? Blockbuster video games already outperform blockbuster movies, so how long until video games look better than movies?

At the time I'm writing this, over six billion hours of video are watched on YouTube every month. That's about an hour for every human on earth, and that is simply one website. Throw in Hulu, Netflix, and the millions of other sites. Then toss in the legacy television networks and hundreds of cable networks. People in the developed world (and not just a few in the undeveloped world) are watching at least five to six hours of some kind of video a day.

Think it doesn't matter, since you're only a consumer right now and not a creator? The future of advertising for your brand will be tied up in innovations in visual experiences. No one's immune. When something changes in the video world, it impacts the entire world.

January 5, 2017

"Mario, what is this Dr Pepper doing in the fridge? You promised me you were giving up sodas and would stick to your diet until you lost the extra ten pounds you put on over the holidays!"

"It's not my fault. The refrigerator just reordered like it always does!"

"You didn't tell the refrigerator about your diet?"

Smart appliances won't just change retail, but the entire buying process. As these thinking appliances proliferate, fortunes will be made by the companies that figure out how to handle orders, fulfillment, and marketing. And like all business, follow the money trail.

As I'm writing this, Google just announced a new credit card that will be tied to your Google wallet. And Coin is taking orders for a new card, which can be loaded with multiple credit and debit cards; you simply select one with a slight turn on a dial with your finger. Developments like Apple Pay threaten all of these. Digital currencies like BitCoin and others are challenging our most basic assumptions and premises about money.

Is the thinking in the C-suites of Macy's, Best Buy, and Home Depot ready for the changes coming in retail? Are the executives in the banking industry ready for the changes in payments? I certainly hope so, but I doubt it. Chances are, at each of these places, there's a person far down the management chain that no one is listening to, even though she is running around with her hair on fire trying to get people on top of these changes. And she'll eventually be the CEO—of the competitor that disrupts them.

September 14, 2024

Out-of-work National Football League player Dennis Smith got the tone indicating he had an incoming communication. He blinked twice quickly to see who it was from and was delighted to see his agent's pic pop up in his video stream. He blinked twice quickly again to answer. Without waiting for a hello, he said, "See, I told you someone would pick me up for the season. With all the advances in medicine today, forty-eight years old is still young for a professional athlete. So who's interested?"

"Easy, Tiger, it's not what you think," his agent replied. "I have an offer from old man Jessup from the Cowboys, but it's not to play again."

"So what does he want?"

"I'm not sure how to say this. He, ah . . . He, ah . . . ."

"What?"

"OK, let me just say it: He knows you haven't been smart with your money. And he doesn't need you to play. He's got young guys now who are half bionic. But he has a very unusual offer for you."

"What? Come on already."

"Well, he knows from the times he spent in the locker room how well endowed you are . . . and . . . he wants . . . your penis. It's a status symbol, and he's willing to pay eighty million credits if you're willing to do a transplant with him. And another five million credits to sign a nondisclosure and keep it secret."

If that sounds farfetched to you, you're not really thinking about the speed of the advances in transplants, technology, and medicine. And what happens when fantasies are obtainable realities? (Not to mention what happens when vapid people get large amounts of riches.)

We've already seen the first hand, leg, and face transplants, and we've been transplanting organs for decades. The first human organs have now been created with 3D printers. This is a field (and area of commerce) that is just beginning to heat up.

Remember: If it's not this, it'll be something else. The greatest opportunities will be recognizing what the something else will be.

March 11, 2026

Brussels, Belgium

As widely speculated, today Marc Bernal, president of the International Olympic Committee, announced that the Olympics will shut down after this year's competition. Trying to administer a fair competition between cloned athletes, transgender and intersex athletes, those who have undergone transplant surgery to improve performance, and athletes with varying degrees of bionic components has made running an impartial contest a nightmare, lowered holovision ratings, and made securing corporate sponsors almost impossible.

Transplants, cloning, and biogenetic engineering won't just change the dynamics of sporting competitions. They will revolutionize medical care, longevity, and retirement, affecting a variety of things from what it means to be human to the businesses of agriculture and insurance, to name just a few.

Take retirement, for instance. For years financial planners have advised their clients to save a small percentage of their income and invest it. But that was when people lived seven or ten years after the time they retired. Now people are living thirty years after retirement. When that number moves to fifty (or two hundred or never), it will require serious rethinking. The longer your time frame is after you stop earning, the greater the danger that inflation will threaten your financial security. Of course, eventually the age at which we retire will be adjusted up dramatically. But for the transition generation or two, there will be previously unseen and serious threats to their financial security. And some delicious opportunities for entrepreneurs.

There is a growing movement made up of people who have built their own electronic brain-stimulation machines. An Atlanta physician named James Fugedy is one of the leaders of the movement, and most of the adherents have the technological savvy to build their own machines. They all report enhanced memory and concentration.

Self-taught biogerontologist Aubrey de Grey created quite a controversy when he suggested the first human beings who will live to a thousand years old have already been born. De Grey makes the case that aging is simply another disease that will be cured.

The approach de Grey uses is to treat aging as an engineering problem, identifying all the components that cause human tissue to age, and then designing remedies for each of them. He has dubbed this process Strategies for Engineered Negligible Senescence (SENS).

Before you discount de Grey as a kook, you should know he's been published in many respected journals. And while many have challenged his assertions, no one has convincingly disputed them.

You probably saw *Transcendence*, the 2014 sci-fi thriller starring Johnny Depp. But how futuristic is that movie really? Ray Kurzweil predicts that we'll be uploading our entire minds to computers by 2045, and machines will replace our fragile bodies within ninety years. Oh, and by the way, that would pretty much make you immortal.

What we're witnessing here is the movement of genetic engineering from the medical world to the personal healthcare market.

This will be similar in scope to what happened when computers moved from business to personal and the Internet went from educational institutions to virtually everyone. This metamorphosis created untold numbers of millionaires and billionaires. Yet that pales in comparison to what will happen when genetics makes this jump.

> **August 13, 2024**
>
> "Danny, I just got your progress update, and you're failing your nine-month online certification!"
>
> "It's no big deal, Mom. I'm sure I'll improve before the final certifications are issued."
>
> "It is a big deal. If you don't pass this, you're going to have to go to college and get an MBA degree. If you have to settle for a college degree, you'll never get a good job, and you'll make less money for the rest of your life."

This may be the most critical issue we will have to deal with: relearning how to learn. If we actually were able to jump into that DeLorean DMC-12 (or perhaps that hot tub time machine), travel back to the eighteenth century, and bring back Immanuel Kant, Thomas Jefferson, or Adam Smith, there is one thing they would immediately recognize: our education system.

Three centuries later, we're still following the same educational model they used back then, one that was designed to train people to work in factories or on farms.

There are flickers of innovation here and there. For example, I am awarding special bonus points for the Management Information Systems Department of the Temple University Fox School of Business and Management, which has, in essence, brought gamification to college. The school has implemented a point system by which students need to achieve a certain amount of professional development points before they can graduate. They promote this with a leaderboard that showcases the students with the most points and by issuing professional achievement badges for the students.

Other than these flickers of creativity and the movement toward online learning, education is still stuck in thinking that's three centuries old. Is it any wonder that so many executives who were trained in our business schools exhibit such derivative, corporate, and herd mentality thinking today?

Simply making the leap from training knowledge workers instead of factory workers would be huge, but that's still not enough. We have to (get to) rethink the role and value of acquiring knowledge.

Of all the industries and professions we've discussed thus far, perhaps none will face such cataclysmic change and be open to more opportunities than education.

Think about the people in charge of helping us think.

Online dating, virtual reality companions, and virtual reality sex situations (and likely cloned sex workers) will completely perplex millions of people with issues relating to intimacy, social interaction, relationships, and addiction. This will present huge new growth opportunities for teachers, professors, relationship therapists, psychiatrists, psychologists, mental health counselors, addiction specialists, and the entire mental health field to develop and grow. But it won't happen at the current level of thinking.

A majority of corporate and thought leaders will be the product of learning and education programs outside of traditional universities. The seemingly infinite warehouse of knowledge stored electronically will disrupt education in momentous ways.

Will the time really come when a college degree is a fallback option for people who couldn't cut it in some kind of specific online vocational certification? Will we reach a point when a six- or nine-month certification in some area from some entity (might be a university, might not be) will be infinitely more valuable than an MBA or even a PhD?

These questions will require thinking much bigger than debating campus versus online learning or traditional universities versus Massive Open Online Courses (MOOCs). The discussion needs to focus instead on issues such as the definition of learning, how we learn, and what learning is actually useful and necessary. Information wants to be free, but the cost of education is headed in the opposite direction.

Here in the United States, the federal government has increased the money it is spending on grants, loans, and tuition tax breaks. Yet the *Wall Street Journal* reports that the average cost of in-state tuition and room and board at a public university has increased 40 percent faster than economy-wide inflation over the last decade. While private school tuition and related costs have not gone up as rapidly, they, too, have outpaced inflation. And, of course, they were much pricier to begin with. The amount of debt required for most people to get a college education today is obscene. The marketability of a degree wanes, the cost continues to rise, and its actual viability and value in the employment market is diminishing.

Like healthcare, entertainment, and other industries, higher learning today is infected with a centuries-old culture that blocks technology and other developments that would improve productivity and effectiveness.

Right now, companies are at the mercy of selecting graduates from business schools that are stuck in an outdated learning model. Savvy employers will have to take a more proactive role in training and education, and savvy employees will have to take more personal responsibility in their own learning.

Of course, there is another, less talked about but critical area to consider: the emotional and philosophical maturation process that can take place while attending university. Nido Qubein, president of High Point University, drives home the point, telling me, "One reality will always exist: Innovation at every corner is a must. But also acknowledging that eighteen-year-olds go to college residentially for an extended period of time also to grow emotionally and mature intellectually. You can't access that through MOOCs."

About the future of higher education, he predicts, "Many colleges will sadly suffer. Some will be enhanced in measurable ways. Along the way, everybody in education must be committed to rethink and re-create how knowledge and wisdom are taught/learned. I do not see a doomsday scenario. I do see a major redo."

Qubein has an optimistic view on the future of education.

But most learning institutions are in the nonprofit or government sector—areas that have traditionally been years behind the private sector in development.

Not only will these institutions have to catch up with the level of thinking in the entrepreneurial world but they will need to stay abreast of the level of thinking needed to jump to in the next decade. This will require an exponential leap.

If I were running Google or Apple right now, the first thing I would do is set aside $50 million to start our own high school and university and begin offering housing, internships, and scholarships to the most talented and promising teens in the world. I wouldn't wait for the education system to catch up with the programs needed to prepare our workforce for success. I would create them. By coming at the situation absent the preconceived memes of the current education model, you could truly create the ideal one.

January 7, 2026

[*Clock ticking audio*] Coming up on *60 Minutes*: We look back on one of the most popular business books of the last decade, *Mad Genius*. When it was first published in 2016, it created quite a stir because of its bold predictions for the decade. Tonight we'll show how far off author Randy Gage was and try to figure out how he could have been so wrong.

OK, it probably won't be *60 Minutes*. But you can be sure ten years from now some media outlet will be licking its chops for the chance to post snarky comments on what I got wrong. I can handle that.

And the reason I can handle it is because *I am supposed to be wrong*. So are you. If you want to win, you have to be willing to fail. You won't get everything right; no one does. Every one of these areas is almost certainly off limits for discussion at the place you currently work. That's how we know these are the places the real money will be made. The entrepreneurs who have the guts to think differently, blow up the box, and tap their Mad Genius have the best odds for success.

Whether you are in any of the businesses mentioned so far or thousands of others I haven't named, you and your business are not prepared for this future.

That's because no one is prepared for all this.

Perhaps some of what I have written has made you mad, sad, or scared. I hope so, because if not, I haven't done my job.

My goal is not to leave you in that state, but to awaken you to the challenges coming and help you prepare for the new and higher level of thinking we must practice—the kind of thinking that will empower, liberate, and energize you. Because once you understand the choices you will be facing and realize the power you have in those choices, the more powerful those choices will become.

The entrepreneurs and companies who help people cope with the cataclysmic changes we're about to face will become the wealthiest on the planet. And probably a few other planets.

But let's dig deeper.

I hesitated to use the phrase *cope with* in the previous paragraphs because it implies that all changes are hurtful and negative. *Coping* usually means dealing with something beyond your control, something being done to you. That's a fundamental problem today: We're all being "done to"—by politicians, educators, and government. Coping is a reactive approach to managing problems, all about looking backward and not being on the level of thinking that will move us toward where we really want to go.

The reality is that many of the changes we're about to experience will be cathartic, liberating, and transformative. The greatest future lies in wait for those who create and ignite this (r)evolution in the first place.

But that's going to require a very different mindset from what they're teaching in most MBA programs. You don't need a new mission statement, another trust fall workshop, or a consultant telling you to "delight and amaze" your customers to do that. You won't do it reading more books about how Starbucks, Zappos, Southwest Airlines, or Nordstrom did it either. You do it by tapping into your Mad Genius as an artist and entrepreneur. You do it when you commit to thinking differently.

You can't just think out of the box, out of this world, or even out of the universe. You've got to think in ways no human being has ever thought before. You've got to create art. Not just any art . . .

You've got to create art that is thermofuckingnuclear!

BOOK THREE

The Age of the Entrepreneur

WHY DOES GRANDMA CUT THE ENDS OFF THE HAM BEFORE SHE PUTS IT IN THE OVEN?

If you had a dime for every motivational speaker giving book reports on the latest hardcover from Jack Welch, Tom Peters, or Jim Collins, you could buy half of Dubai. But you don't really need another bestseller summary, do you?

Likewise for all the consultants and speakers who give those speeches about getting out of the box, Roger Bannister and the four-minute mile, or why Grandma cut the ends off the ham/turkey/roast beef before she put it in the oven. And do you really need to hear the starfish story again?

Unfortunately, the speakers and consultants sharing those lessons have fallen prey to the very thing they're preaching against: *habitual thinking*.

And nothing does more to dumb you down, hold you back, and prevent you from creative thinking than getting mired in a stale thought pattern. It's the ultimate limiting belief, because it precludes most possibility thinking.

The smarter you are, the greater the likelihood you are intellectually lazy. Don't be.

NURTURING YOUR
MAD GENIUS

What's the secret to getting in front of trends, seeing around the corner, and being the first mover in lucrative new markets? How can you unleash the awesome brilliance you have inside, waiting to bubble over? Just how do you tap into your innate Mad Genius to create breakthrough marketing, innovate new products, or develop fresh concepts?

Well, let's start with the bad news. If you're the bottom line, action-oriented, results type in those personality profile tests (you know who you are), you're in for a disappointment. I don't have an exact, top-secret, patent-pending, seven-step process for developing Mad Genius to sell you. (And if I did, I certainly wouldn't sell it to you for the special, one-time-only, introductory offer, operators are standing by now, ridiculously low price of this manifesto.) Know this:

The path to thermofuckingnuclear is not a linear one.

The process, and even the environment, for developing breakthrough products, disrupting markets, and creating brilliant concepts is often a wild, circuitous one. Sometimes it means bouncing off the walls like a pinball. Other times it means finding inspiration in the shower, playing the "what if" game, discovering the 999 ways it doesn't work, and sometimes—amazingly enough—when you're actually trying to come up with an idea for something.

Many of you reading this have a team you want to inspire and empower to embrace creative, possibility thinking. Others of you are solopreneurs looking for the one thing that will bust you through to success. In either case, Mad Genius begins with you. And yes, you do possess Mad Genius. Everyone does. It simply manifests itself differently, depending on your environment, experiences, and how you nurture it—or don't.

What I'm about to share with you is everything I know about unleashing Mad Genius. I'll try to be as concise as possible. You're busy, I'm busy, and we both know that the more time you spend *reading* about how to tap into your creative brilliance translates into less time you're actually *being* creatively brilliant.

I'll be positive and encouraging because I love the subject and the creative high that comes with helping people create art and become amazing. But know that while I believe everyone has the gift of genius, it isn't something you find. It's a process you commit to. You're going to have to do the work. And achieving any breakthrough starts with a decision.

So if you have decided you want to be one of the cool kids, allow me to share some insights on what it takes to become a critical thinker and see the world and its possibilities in bold and breathtaking new ways.

First, you have to be doing work that matters to you. It doesn't have to be important to everyone, but it better be important to you. Nothing dumbs down and dampens creativity like wasting it in the pursuit of mediocrity. Attempt epic things that are so intoxicating they pull you toward them. It may or may not be work that changes the world, but it better change *your* state. It should bring you joy, ignite your passion, or bring you harmony.

I had the honor of dining with one of my heroes, legendary

tenor Plácido Domingo. Of course, he's one of the greatest artists of all time, a brilliant conductor, a worldwide icon, and the recipient of a dozen Grammys. But there's one thing about him I find most fascinating.

Most opera singers at a world-class level like Domingo are known for a few signature roles. They find the ones that best match their language, style, and vocal range. Then they spend the rest of their career making the circuit of the various opera houses around the world, sticking to the three or four roles they're famous for.

Domingo doesn't perform four—he performs 134.

This is simply unheard of for someone operating at his level. So I asked him what drove him to do that. Did he get bored with being safe? Does he do it because he seeks the challenge? His answer was surprising.

"It's nothing to do with challenge," he replied in a voice as lyrical speaking as it is singing. "I have passion for the music. And even if I lived three lifetimes, I could never perform all the music I love!"

When you have the same joyfulness to bring your product to market, launch your new venture, or create the next breakthrough concept, you'll power your own creativity.

THE PROBLEM WITH PROBLEM SOLVING

When dealing with any challenge or setback, consider your frame of reference and the context of the discussion. Often the premise is misstated, and if the premise is wrong, everything that comes from that premise is wrong.

If you charge your team with solving a problem, you shouldn't be surprised to discover later that they have been looking backward. Problem solving in and of itself is inherently backward looking.

For real breakthroughs you have to stop living in the problem and live in the solution instead.

The same holds true if you're instructing your team to solve a puzzle. Jigsaw puzzles work because all the pieces are in the box when you buy them; all you have to do is figure out where to place each piece.

However, as you saw in Book Two, all the necessary pieces for the challenges you and your business are about to face aren't in the box. So if we're going to use the puzzle analogy here, we have to modify the parameters. Now your job is to use all the puzzle pieces that came in the box, see where they fit, then fill the remaining space by creating some new pieces in that 3D printer called your brain.

When you empower your team to create a possibility, a whole different, forward-looking perspective is created. What we're really talking about is your ability to see the intangible. Let me give you a real-world example how this plays out in the entrepreneurial space.

I was approached by Linius, a tech start-up, to serve on their advisory board. One of their existing board members had read my book *Risky Is the New Safe* and suggested they bring me onboard because I knew where tech and video were heading.

I spent a day floundering around their website and still had no clue what it was they actually did. So I emailed a few of my really smart colleagues in an Internet mastermind group I belong to, asking for their take. They came back with similar bewilderment.

These colleagues are really bright people, all successful entrepreneurs who harness the Internet and have built huge businesses on it. They didn't see any marketable value in the technology Linius offered either.

But a feeling kept gnawing at me.

I felt like something was there, if only I could quantify it in a way I could wrap my mind around. I'm no techie by any stretch of the imagination. I don't know how to write code and have a hard enough time recording two programs simultaneously on a DVR.

My gift is not in understanding what makes technology work, but how humans use technology and, most importantly, how that technology can solve problems and create possibilities. Because . . .

When you know how to solve problems, then you know how to create wealth. And when you know how to see and act on possibilities, then you know how to create disproportionate wealth.

Entrepreneurs with the ability to solve problems get rich. Entrepreneurs with the ability to envision as yet unseen possibilities get really, really rich.

The iPad didn't really solve a problem and no one was asking for it. Steve Jobs envisioned a possibility for something that, once people were exposed to it, they simply had to have.

So I kept exploring what it was that Linius did and pondering why anyone else would care. It took me a couple days longer to understand that what founder Finbar O'Hanlon had actually done was create a language for video known as VQL, for video query language. (Which, of course, Finbar already knew but couldn't explain to me due to the language difference: I speak English and he speaks tech.)

Now I had a concept my high school dropout mind could actually process.

Larry Ellison created a language for data, and that made Oracle worth $37 billion—give or take a few billion. So that led me to believe that a language for video might have some intrinsic value in the marketplace.

When video is turned into a language, transcoding is no longer necessary. A video query language would mean any business in the world could use the data they or other companies possess to dynamically build content. Data at every frame can be disassembled, reassembled, and reordered in seconds without any processing.

That language could allow Google to apply their AdSense program to their YouTube channel with ferocious velocity. Or networks such as FOX, CNN, and BBC could unlock the value in their content by extracting specific frames of audio and video out of a single file, then publish this extract as part of a new show, without having to go to an edit suite.

Because I began to see potential uses for the technology, I went back to my brilliant Internet mastermind partners. But now when I presented the question, I was doing so in a context that some of them could immediately grasp. They suggested even more uses for the technology than I had envisioned.

The promise of such a system would mean revolutionizing how we watch video. For example, suppose you have a video that shows a number of different kinds of pets, but you want to view only those clips featuring dogs. Instead of having to cut and edit a very long video into a new video montage of the dog segments, you could use the indexing system to simply select and play those segments, creating a new video on-the-fly. Going to extremes, a NASCAR fan in Nashville could set his feed to follow only a specific car, rather than all drivers.

Or as another example, a network (broadcast or otherwise) could stream one feed of a movie or program around the globe but still offer different versions: the NC-17-rated one to a single guy in New York with the latest NTSC smart TV; someone in Auckland watching in PAL format; and a family in Abu Dhabi watching the version with adult content filtered out. All from the same stream.

The reception device would determine what data to pick from the stream and display. The control could be at the user's end or, more likely, at the service provider's end, with the ability to exercise that control for an additional fee.

The potential for disruption is staggering—in fields from sports to news, entertainment to law enforcement, encryption to even national security.

The true value of the concept, and all the others we'll look at in this book, will be determined by the market. Like any start-up, Linius could go big or go bust, and the eventual outcome will have to be played out in the actual marketplace.

As is the case with most new ventures, success then becomes about the strength of the patents, adequate financing, a talented start-up team, and other variables. But the real lesson here is your ability to see possibilities.

THE REALITY OF MIRACLES

It doesn't take much insight to know there's money to be made selling lemonade in the desert. Mad Genius is the ability to think creatively and see opportunities that aren't so obvious. That's where the greatest opportunities lie in wait.

Verdant Technologies LLC in Scottsdale, Arizona, is conducting research on how changing the frequency of liquids and solids can enable them to do things they couldn't normally do. This actually changes the molecular structure of the target material, thus changing the results you get. In their tests so far, they are producing 40 percent higher crop yields in fields and greenhouses by changing the frequency of water. Other experiments have shown 15 percent stronger concrete, batteries that recharge faster and last longer, and magnets that are strengthened more than 30 percent.

The company faces skepticism because, to many, this kind of transformation sounds like a miracle. Of course, in a way it is, because all physics is a miracle.

WHAT NEW REALITIES (POSSIBILITIES) DO YOU WANT?

Ian Percy is an organizational psychologist with a business card that identifies him as a *Possibility Coach*. (OK, does anyone actually have business cards anymore? But that's his job title.) He brought several tech geniuses together in a start-up called Emendara LLC that is focused on not one but two "impossibilities."

First, they claim to possess technology capable of locating *all* faults and errors in software. The number of people in the world who currently believe in even the *possibility* of fault-free software can probably be counted on one hand.

Second, two members of the group patented a new "massively parallel processor"—a superchip that can process a breathtaking 65,536 bits per cycle. (Currently a typical chip in your computer processes 128 bits per cycle.)

Forget Moore's Law. This is a leap in several levels of magnitude in processing power, and the implications are staggering. Put both these "impossibilities" together, and it's estimated that they'll be able to find all faults in thirty million lines of software code in fewer than ten minutes.

But when Percy presented the concept to seasoned, high-level technocrats, he was often greeted with utter disbelief and waved off without a discussion. And that still happens, even though the existence of this superchip—now called the Automata Processor—has been announced by Micron Technologies and will likely already be released by the time you're reading this.

Here's the real takeaway: Many of the possibilities emerging now—and others that will emerge—are such exponential advancements that many people, even highly educated ones, can't understand them, so they initially discount their validity. Most of us have been conditioned to linear, incremental advancements. *Now we're moving into an age of exponential innovations, and many people are simply not mentally prepared to deal with these huge leaps.*

This is vividly demonstrated by the rash of recent TED videos (from the real conference, not the one I made up earlier) in which teenagers are coming up with incredible technical and biological discoveries that are shaking up the established scientific community.

Seventeen-year-old Angela Zhang produced research that might lead to a potential cure for cancer. Teenager Jack Andraka developed an early detection system for pancreatic cancer that is twenty-eight times faster than current tests. Samantha Garvey, homeless at the time, was recognized for her discoveries in marine biology. High school senior Eric Chen was awarded a scholarship for his work that might prevent flu outbreaks. Like a lot of geniuses, they are too naive to know why something won't work. Are you?

MOVING
FROM BEHIND
TO BEYOND

Regardless of what happens with any of these ventures, they illustrate the complexity of the issues we will be facing and the type of thinking they will require.

Problem solving, by its very nature, is reactive. We're going to need to move away from that thought process and move toward being able to recognize the opportunities inherent in challenges. The possibility-thinking model is really the only way forward—so that we can synergistically coexist with the machines and continue our own onward evolution.

Simply solving problems is a mindset geared to the past. Creating possibilities is a mindset to the future—creating that future.

I'm not sure there were ever any set rules for entrepreneurs and leaders, but if there were, they're all out the window now. Because . . .

We are entering the decade of chaos.

And chaos isn't always a bad thing. Sometimes it's downright delicious.

In evolutionary processes such as many we are discussing in this book, order (the opposite of chaos) is actually increasing. But the catalyst for this order was initially chaos. That's because order itself is a natural state, baked in the cake by Mother Nature.

From the ultimate chaos of the Big Bang, gasses cooled, planets emerged, gravity developed, solar systems coalesced, creatures crawled from the swamp, apes began to walk upright, and eventually U2 recorded "Where the Streets Have No Name."

Chaos creates order and order then builds on itself, which will eventually lead to a seminal milestone: technology creating its own next generation without any intervention from us, the species that created it.

Some of what we're talking about could best be described as *chaortic*, the term Ian Percy uses to label the delicate dance between order and chaos. In fact, if you think about some of the case studies we just looked at, there is nothing chaotic about them, other than that they defy conventional expectations of order. In reality, they ultimately bring order to things. The (r)evolution of technological advancement is accelerating exponentially, because it builds on its own increasing order. Developing your own creative genius often follows a similar process.

Some creativity is *adaptive*—modifying or altering what already exists in new ways. Other creativity is *innovative*—introducing something entirely new that had not existed before. Either one can make you wealthy, and either one can change the world.

WHOLE-BRAIN
SYNCHRONICITY

One of the first things you can do to develop your own Mad Genius is to stop classifying your brain into left–right or logical–creative sides. Likewise, stop categorizing yourself in one group or the other. These beliefs about the two different sides of brain function come from research done with accident or stroke victims who have lost the use of parts of their brain. If you've read this far, you're still accessing enough from both sides of your brain to be brilliant.

The optimal state for you is what scientists call whole-brain synchronicity, in which you have thoughts going back and forth, creating neural pathways between the right and left hemispheres of your brain.

This synchronicity between the two halves of the brain dramatically improves your creative powers, not to mention your learning ability, memory, and intuition. It is believed this increased communication between the two hemispheres is what separates geniuses like Einstein, Edison, and Mozart from the average person.

Once you pry open the rusty gate between the two halves of your brain, you start to experience:

- Increased mental clarity
- Greater creativity
- Improved learning ability

THE CREATIVITY
TRIAD

Three things are necessary to foster creative genius: *experience*, some form of a *capturing system*, and *taking action*. Let's look at each.

The experiences you go through provide the stimulation that jump-starts your creativity. This is why most people aren't creative. They do the same thing, day after day. They work in the same dead-end job for years, eat at the same restaurants, ordering the same entrée, and vacation at the same place every year. They have a standardized, limited spectrum of experiences.

Creative people travel, learn new languages, study other cultures, and meet many different people. Their lives are a kaleidoscope of many interesting and different experiences. And because each day offers new experiences, neural pathways don't grind ruts in their brain. They aren't so susceptible to habitual thinking and are much more likely to attain a self-actualized state.

The other thing that creative people do is to capture their experiences and internalize them. That's why so many creative people are speakers, writers, musicians, actors, and, of course, entrepreneurs. Actors like Al Pacino, Meryl Streep, and Denzel Washington lose themselves in a role. They are subconsciously capturing the emotion of the situation they are acting out. Only they aren't acting anymore; they are living in the role. A creative writing genius like Hemingway captured the ethos, emotion, and physical context of the situations he wrote about. He put himself into the situation and then brought us along for the ride.

It's probably not a coincidence that many of the most brilliant entrepreneurs I know—who are loaded down with smartphones, tablets, and laptops—still have a paper journal they physically write in. Journaling can really stoke your creative muse. It does so because it keeps you alone with your thoughts. This type of mental seclusion and introspection is always good for creation. (I have two desks: a regular one with technology on it and also a drafting table with nothing but poster board, sketchpads, and colored pencils and markers.)

The best way to capture concepts, however, is to create them.

That's where taking action comes in. Imagination by itself is not creativity. Creativity requires that you actually do something with what you're daydreaming about. Start that company, launch that new product, develop that innovative app.

Not everything you try will work, but that's not the point. The point is that you're in the game, doing things, moving forward. You'll learn as much or more from your failures as you will from your successes. Celebrate it all.

> Newtonian physics has taken you as far as it can.
> The economy is now rewarding art and innovation
> and guts . . . brilliant ideas executed with singular
> direction by aligned teams on behalf of truly
> motivated customers. Take the intellectual risks and
> do the emotional labor you're capable of.
>
> —Seth Godin

FIGHTING THE DISEASE OF BIG

If you remember the great recession of 2008, there was a lot of talk about the big banks and investment houses being "too big to fail." That's debatable, but there is no debate that banks offer way too many examples of something every successful entrepreneur must guard against: becoming too big to excel.

This happens when organizations reach success and add too many layers, doctrines, and bureaucracy. Much like book publishers who seem determined to make themselves irrelevant, banking is another industry that seems oblivious to the threats it is facing. Too big can quickly turn into irrelevant.

Let me share a case study of exactly how the banking industry works, as it contains numerous lessons on how organizations get so big that they can no longer respond and stay competitive in the marketplace.

During my recent sabbatical, I was traveling the world and thought it might be cool to pick somewhere on a map and move there. I always enjoyed San Diego when I visited there, so decided to relocate there if the right place became available.

I contacted my banker at Wells Fargo and told him I wanted to get preapproval for a mortgage, so if I found something I liked, I could close immediately. I gave him an amount, submitted all the documents they requested, and a month later got an approval. (Which should have been the first alarm. A month is a ridiculous waiting time in today's market.)

I engaged a local real estate broker and found a building I liked a lot, but there were no units on a high floor with the view I wanted. A few months later, while I was living in Australia, a unit meeting my criteria became available on short notice.

The San Diego market was hot. I wanted to close fast. Units went into whisper listings and were sold in days. But Wells Fargo was still living in the real estate bubble meltdown days. For six weeks I tried every day to close. For six weeks, every day they asked for another document, another letter, or another something. Remember, this was all after I was already "preapproved."

So what was the issue? There was a lawsuit between the homeowners association and the developer. Not an unusual occurrence today. In fact, quite common. I knew of the lawsuit when I made the offer and had no problem with it. The developer was cooperating with the association to help reach a settlement with the insurance company.

But because the litigation existed, whoever was allegedly empowered to make the decision couldn't tick that box on the checklist. So for six weeks they sent a steady stream of requests for more information with no end in sight. I finally gave up in exasperation, sold some of my precious metals, and paid cash for the apartment.

Banks (or any business) can't get away with operating that way in today's market if they want to stay relevant. But we're just getting started on this little case study.

I decided Wells Fargo was simply too bureaucratic in nature to be a viable bank for an entrepreneur like me. But just when I was ready to close all my accounts, I discovered they were the major donor to the San Diego Asian Film Festival, an event near and dear to my heart. So I kept my business with them.

Fast-forward to a year later.

I realize the "throw a dart on the map" method of where to live does not take into account the income tax ramifications. California has some of the most onerous, repressive, and stifling income tax codes in the United States. So I decide to spend only the summers there and make Florida my primary residency again.

I find a beautiful penthouse I like, and once again, the market is hot. In fact, the Miami market is blistering. And once again, the banks are clueless to the reality of the current situation. Trying to be clever this time around, I go to LendingTree where "banks fight for your business."

True enough, within minutes I have fifteen lenders sending me email pitches, including of course, Wells Fargo. Now a couple things you should know before we go further . . .

I probably have about the highest credit score you can have for anyone not named Bill Gates or Oprah. I have zero debt, own everything outright, and I make a lot of money. I have at least five credit cards with over $50,000 or unlimited limits, all of which I pay in full every month. I'm the ideal target customer for any bank.

I start the process of applying for a mortgage with all the lenders from LendingTree. Well, it turns out the building I want to buy in opened in 2009, during the bubble burst. There were many speculators in the building and lots of foreclosures, so now the building is unwarrantable, with neither Freddie Mac nor Fannie Mae willing to guarantee loans in the building.

Thirteen of the fifteen lenders immediately disqualify themselves. They're still living in the 2009 market, oblivious to the extraordinary opportunities the 2014 Miami market is offering them. (Or the lucrative new customer they could land.) It comes down to Citibank and my old friends at Wells Fargo.

I call the guy who has emailed me from Wells Fargo, explain my disdain for the last time I attempted a mortgage with them, and tell him not to waste either of our time if he can't turn around an approval quickly. He is actually a conscientious, well-meaning guy and implores me to give him a chance to make things right with the bank.

Once he finds out the building isn't warrantable, he knows he's in trouble. He tells me, "This loan is no good to the bank, because they can't sell it." Keep in mind, I'm a sixteen-year customer with Wells Fargo and move millions of dollars through my accounts. I get that Wells Fargo or any bank needs to make a profit off my business to survive. I'm a free market guy and have no problem with that. But can't they at least maintain the facade that they want to service my financial needs and keep me as a customer?

Because what was my account rep really telling me?

If we put what he told me into Google translate, it would come back as, "Sorry, Randy, the interest rate we would make on your loan isn't enough to satisfy us. If we can't flip your loan and gouge some extra money off you, we really couldn't care less about keeping you as a customer."

Still my heroic rep wanted to get the deal done and insisted he could get a waiver for the building. Unfortunately the situation turned into *Groundhog Day*. Every day, endless requests for trivial and irrelevant documents. Things like this: They would see a large direct deposit from XYZ company in my bank account, and they would ask for a letter from XYZ company verifying that they had really sent the deposit. Even though the money was in the account, and that company has been sending me monthly direct deposits for more than nine years.

They wanted three years of tax returns, so I sent them. Three weeks later they said they needed them certified. So my accountant literally drove the completed forms over to the IRS and waited there until they could do that. Four weeks later, Wells Fargo then said they needed transcripts of the returns to make sure I hadn't exaggerated my income. (Obviously there must be an epidemic of people filing tax returns claiming extra income so they can pay more taxes, probably in a patriotic attempt to bring down the deficit. When I suggested that to my rep, he replied it was just standard practice now to always get transcripts. So why didn't they just request them eight weeks earlier, I asked. Awkward silence.)

I wanted to close in two or three weeks. Wells Fargo couldn't get an answer—approval or denial in eight weeks when the closing was scheduled and I would lose my earnest money deposit. At the last minute I got a one-week extension from the seller. Wells Fargo still couldn't give me answer, only requests for more documentation. Once again, there was a box that couldn't be checked on the checklist and simply no process in place for an actual thinking human being to make a decision.

Come deadline day, the poor guy handling my account was

too embarrassed to even contact me anymore. He's the perfect example of a great employee choking in a dead organization. (And this is happening in thousands of organizations today.)

Which left me down to just Citi.

Turns out they're no better than Wells Fargo and are probably worse. Just like with Wells Fargo, I immediately submitted every item on the list they asked for. But like Wells Fargo, Citi doesn't really have a mortgage approval department; they have a mortgage obstruction department. So every few days they ask for additional items not on the original list. Every few days my assistant sends exactly what they ask for. I keep reminding them that my closing deadline is fast approaching. It finally comes down to four days before closing, and they're stuck because they need not only a waiver for the building being unwarrantable, but an additional waiver because of another lawsuit, this time a silly, inconsequential one between the building and the cable provider.

My rep says it shouldn't be a problem. But the four days expire, and they still don't have an answer. Remember, though, I got a week extension. On closing day I tell them I absolutely must have an answer. Either give me the loan or send a letter of denial that they're afraid to lend on the building for the two given reasons and let me try and get my deposit back.

Five o'clock comes and goes. A supervisor emails me that she will be watching the account all night and send me an answer as soon as she hears. (On a Friday night. In the banking industry. Seriously.)

Of course, I never hear a peep. Monday I write again, because now I'm technically in default and at risk of losing $30,000. They assure me they have escalated the file to the highest-level executive to get me an answer right away. The whole day passes without a word from them. The seller calls my title agent and demands she release my $30,000 deposit to them.

I send one final email to Citi the next morning. I explain the severity of the situation again and let them know I can't process any more frustration and emotional distress from Citi not being able to give a simple answer on a loan request in a timely and professional matter.

I remind them that I'm actually looking for more than a mortgage. What I'm really looking for is a bank and a banker who can handle all of my business needs. I'm an entrepreneur with many ventures, so I require a banker who thinks like an entrepreneur, not an entry-level employee at a fast-food restaurant or a bureaucracy so bloated with mindless procedures that everyone is afraid or unable to make a decision. It shouldn't matter if I was requesting this mortgage to buy a crack house in Overtown or a brothel in Las Vegas. My financial statement, credit score, history, and credit worthiness are solid enough that this should have been a forty-eight-hour decision.

So I make it clear that one of two things has to happen that day: Number one, send me a written approval via email to me and my title agent, giving rates and what time the funds will be in my account. Or number two, send me a letter of denial based on their fear of financing in the building because it is unwarrantable and has the lawsuit, so that I can make an attempt to get my deposit back.

I close with these exact words: "Let me make this very clear: These are the *only* two options available. Sending me another message that the process is continuing and a decision hasn't been reached is not acceptable. I need to have the funds available by tomorrow so I can make one last effort with the seller that they will accept the deal and not attempt to seize my earnest money deposit. Or I need your letter of denial so I can attempt to get my deposit back and hope your bad faith actions in this matter have not cost me $30,000."

At 10 a.m. Pacific Standard Time, my rep from Citi responds with a reply stating, "I have to offer my apologies as we aren't in a position to meet the first option at this time. We are unable to proceed with any type of approval without requesting additional documentation from you."

And the additional documentation they were requesting?

- A letter stating why I owned some property in Florida (that I didn't own).
- A signed/dated letter that the tenant in the property I was buying would be vacating the property. (There was no tenant.)
- A copy of the lease from that imaginary tenant.
- A detailed letter of explanation, signed and dated, explaining why I moved to California and was now buying in Florida again.

At that point, what can you do? I replied to send me a letter of denial and stop wasting everyone's time. Which leads us to the first lesson in all this:

You can't do business with small-minded people.

There is not a force on earth with enough power to overcome a low-level bureaucrat in a cubicle who wants to kill a deal. If you ever find yourself in this situation, the smart move is to cut your losses and move on. I ate my thirty grand and moved on.

I don't tell you all this just to rant out my frustration with bureaucratic companies that are so clueless they don't realize they are really operating customer prevention departments. (OK, maybe just a little.) Both Wells Fargo and Citi are textbook examples of the kind of organizational thinking and culture that dominate a lot of C-suites in the corporate world today. Yes, the banking industry is particularly infected, but you'll see this kind of backward, bloated, and out-of-touch thinking in a lot of industries. It's the ultimate herd thinking. Any employees with an entrepreneurial mindset in these organizations are driven away, and the only people left are the mindless drones who can only tick boxes on checklists.

You can bet my net worth is higher than 999 of the last 1,000 mortgages both banks have approved. You can bet my credit score is higher than 999 of the last 1,000 mortgages both banks have approved. You can bet my annual income is higher than 999 of the last 1,000 mortgages both banks have approved.

There was no debate to my creditworthiness, character, or ability to repay this loan. But both organizations have a culture of institutionalized stupidity. If every box on the form can't be ticked, there is no one with the ability and latitude to fix the situation and keep the customer. They're not too big to fail, simply too big to excel at anything any longer.

One last note on banking that's worth looking at: The biggest trend in banking these days is the reemergence of small, local banks. But, of course, they won't have any better success than the dinosaurs if they don't think at a higher level either. During the fiasco I was experiencing with Wells Fargo and Citi, my real estate broker suggested we offer a chance at my mortgage to a friend he had at a local bank in Orlando.

My experience there wasn't much different, with delays, red tape, arcane procedures, and a less-than-efficient banker who seemed to be harming more than helping along the process. Now, you are probably thinking it's not exactly breaking news that there is another lazy worker-drone working in the banking industry. I mention it only because of the man's job title. He was the bank's president.

Do you think the banking industry is prepared for the challenges of offshore banks, crypto currencies, Apple Pay, digital wallets, and all the other developments in finance and payments? Of course they're not. We have to question if there really is any purpose for banks in the new economy.

The banking industry is easy to pick on because large institutions like Wells Fargo and Citi operate in an alternate universe (called "the past") where they think they're so big and indispensable they can dictate terms and make their customers jump through hoops to meet their ever-growing need for bureaucracy. But those days (and those types of organizations) won't last. The real issue you should be concerned with is how the culture in your organization stacks up in this regard. Here are some questions to ask about your organization:

- Do you have a process or system in place now that is overcompensating for a market situation that existed one, two, or even five years ago?
- Are your people empowered to make decisions to save a valued customer?

- Have you added so many layers of bureaucracy that you're now out of touch with your market?
- Is your buying process set up to make things easy for your prospects and customers or do you make them jump through hoops to make things easier for your bureaucracy?
- What is the one development that could disrupt your industry and make your organization irrelevant?

NOTE: Seven days *after* the final deadline when I would lose my deposit, my Wells Fargo rep emailed me excitedly to tell me he had an approval . . . if I would just submit another five items. I didn't know whether to scream, eat a banana, or stick my head in the oven.

THE CURIOUS THING ABOUT CURIOSITY

I was in a taxi heading to the Birmingham airport on my way home after a softball tournament. As we rolled up, a sign proclaimed, "Welcome to the Birmingham International Airport." Nothing special, the same kind of sign you see at the entrance to practically every airport everywhere.

But something unusual about that sign intrigued me. Think about it.

I'll wait . . .

I asked the taxi driver what international airline flew into Birmingham, Alabama. He had no idea. So I asked the skycap. No idea. Checked with the counter agent. She didn't know either, but now she was intrigued as well and asked the agent next to her. And the next. Called the supervisor. Not one of them knew. On the eighth agent, we finally got an answer: There was a Delta flight from Atlanta to Birmingham that was a code share with Aeroméxico, thus making Birmingham an "international" airport.

How many hundreds of thousands of travelers have gone past that sign and never wondered about it?

I believe the curiosity that caused me to ask that question and continue pursuing it until answered is the same trait that has made me a successful entrepreneur. The power of curiosity to drive innovation, critical thinking, and creativity cannot be overstated.

CURIOUS,
NOT FURIOUS

Back in 2007 I was asked to deliver a keynote for the National Speakers Association (NSA) convention. The convention organizer was the previously mentioned Ian Percy, and he asked me to speak on the subject of prosperity consciousness. He specifically asked me to challenge the audience (something I love to do) and question any limiting beliefs that I thought were holding them back.

In those days, NSA was a very conservative organization committed to continuing to do things the same ways they had been doing them since the 1970s. There were a lot of talented people there, but most were motivational speakers with cyclical, unstable businesses. (And, unfortunately, a number of not-so-talented people, the ones who were still telling the Bannister four-minute mile, why Grandma cut the ends off of the ham/turkey/roast beef, and starfish story speeches.) The majority of both groups followed the business model of "It's easier to find a new audience than create a new speech."

Looking over the members' websites, it appeared the organization contained 573 people who were the number one sales trainer in the world. There were at least 300 claiming to be the preeminent motivational speaker in the galaxy. And at least a dozen who really could move mountains with a mustard seed. So I challenged the audience with a few relevant questions. Such as:

- If you're such an amazing sales trainer, how come you can't sell more of your speeches?
- If you're such a dynamic motivator, how come you can't motivate speaker bureaus to call you?
- If you're such a successful business development consultant, why don't you just hire yourself?
- If you really can move mountains with a mustard seed, why can't you get Oprah to endorse your book?

I wasn't asking these questions to be snarky. (Not that I'm above being snarky, mind you.) But I did want to point out the incongruities between the skill sets they were selling to their clients and the actual results they were achieving in their own businesses.

But the real place I wanted to take them to was questioning their core beliefs about self-worth and prosperity.

I wanted them to examine what was really holding back their career. Did they simply have the wrong marketing copy, demo video, or website or were they subconsciously self-sabotaging their success due to worthiness issues?

There were about 1,500 people in the room and by this point there was a lot of fidgeting and nervous laughter. But to NSA's credit, at least 1,480 of them were sincerely willing to do the critical thinking and explore the issue. In fact, more than eight years later, I'm still getting letters from people who were in that audience telling me that speech was a seminal turning point for them.

However, there were a couple dozen other people there who were absolutely furious with me. Maybe because of the mustard seed jibe, or perhaps because my Facebook profile lists me as a "fundamentalist agnostic," but they equated me to everything from a heathen to the anti-Christ. Several of them stormed out of the convention hall, slamming the door behind them. And because they make convention hall doors so they don't slam very loudly, one lady actually came back in so she could re-exit and slam it again.

Entrepreneurs don't have the luxury of such closed minds.

We don't even have the luxury of simply objective minds. Please take a breath and read that last sentence again. If you want to really unleash your Mad Genius, you have to be willing to question any and all core foundational beliefs you have. About everything.

Question everything.

You start with being objective. Then become subjective. Then you become unreasonable, and if that still doesn't take you where you need to be, you move on to outrageous.

Question everything.

Beliefs are a really funny thing. Most everyone has some unreasonable and outrageous beliefs, but they believe they're completely sane and sensible. As a result, most people are very averse to questioning their beliefs. But that's where the real breakthroughs live.

Question everything.

It's all about critical thinking, to make sure your beliefs are based on correct premises. It is only by examining, questioning, and then analyzing your beliefs that you can determine if they really serve you.

Question everything.

If your beliefs serve you, you keep them. If you find a belief doesn't serve you, remove it like you would an ill-fitting coat and replace it with one that fits you better. And the next time someone challenges a core belief you hold, try being curious instead of furious.

He says the sky is red. But I know it's really blue. They taught me that in the second grade. I can look out the window right now and see blue sky. So why does he believe the sky is red?

Curiosity comes from inquisitiveness, and being inquisitive is a foundation for creative thinking. By their very nature, brilliant entrepreneurs question everything. "Why is everyone doing it that way?" "Why can't it be done?" "I know it's impossible, but if it were possible, how could we do it?"

Danny Iny, founder of Firepole Marketing, has a fast-growing online business. He tells me:

> From where I'm sitting, the most important foundational factor for entrepreneurial creativity is an attitude of "why we should" and "how we will," as opposed to "whether we should" or "why we can't." I'm not saying that you should run with every hare-brained idea. But you can't know which ideas are really hare-brained and which have that touch of Mad Genius that makes them awesome and at the same time just far enough "out there" for most people to reject them as too complicated or too risky.
>
> The first step to being creative is to say, "Yes, let's do it, here's how we can make it work." Entrepreneurial brainstorming should be conducted like an improv class

(in which the cardinal rule is that you always run with the improvisations of your colleagues, never contradict, and never say no, because that just kills the energy of it all).

Make it a rule in your organization that whenever a new idea is proposed, the first response has to be positive and supportive, cultivating that idea. This can be very difficult, but it's worth it; I don't always succeed, but I've tried very hard to eliminate the knee-jerk "no" from my vocabulary and replace it with "tell me more."

Question everything. Including the idea that you should question everything.

DON'T BUY INTO
THE CONVENTIONAL
BELIEFS

Every industry has its sacred cows and accepted practices. These are based on foundational beliefs, and often those beliefs are based on premises that are no longer valid. (If they ever even were.)

Earlier I said mobile apps won't just change marketing, they will change everything. The reason these apps (and other new business models) can be so disruptive is because they're often created by people who aren't from the industries they're disrupting.

There is a reason Amazon was started by Jeff Bezos and not anyone in the bookstore industry, and Uber was started by people who weren't in the taxi industry. Because they were not in those industries, these pioneers hadn't bought into all the limiting conventional beliefs possessed by most decision makers in the space.

I'm sure lots of people in the taxi industry thought about using GPS systems to route drivers to fares. But because they were stuck in the herd thinking of their industry, they probably threw out the idea as too expensive or not feasible. They were vested in their system of dispatchers and radios, and because they had a monopoly, they felt no urgency to test other models. But the free market blew them up.

When the Kickstarter campaign for the Pebble Time smartwatch raised $8 million in about twelve hours, that was your clue that the rules have changed.

Human nature seems to have a default setting about innovation. Anything in existence when you were born (no matter how stunning of a quantum advancement it was), just seems ordinary and natural to you. Anything new developed when you're in your teens and twenties is breathtaking and revolutionary, and you're excited to be a part of it. And anything developed after you're forty is irritating and evil, because it prevents you from going back to the way things were.

Bookstores thought people would never buy books online, and record companies thought they could ban music downloads. But you can never turn back the clock.

I love a good bookstore as much as anyone, but I still order most of my books from Amazon. I actually still have the original *Dark Side of the Moon* and some other classic LP albums. But 99 percent of my music is on my iPhone.

This is not a cautionary tale of the taxi industry, the bookstore business, or record companies.

It's a wake-up call for every industry. Taxi companies won't beat back ride-sharing apps because they provide great value to consumers and achieved immediate acceptance. Other industries won't defeat disruption in their space because disruption is intrinsically proconsumer. It works only if the marketplace accepts it, and the marketplace accepts it only if it is doing something better, faster, or cheaper. Or all three.

If you're in a business trying to restrict or outlaw an app or business model that threatens you, you're already a dinosaur. You'd be better off working to develop a better app.

Market destruction is tough when you're the collateral damage. But that's the way free enterprise works, and free enterprise is the only way to keep an economy vibrant. It's not about the destruction but rather, the creation that comes from it.

OVERTHROW
THE GOVERNMENT!

OK, we don't really have to overthrow the government. (At least not yet.) But the Internet, mobile apps, and other disruptive developments will continue to force us to change the way we think about the power, scope, and role of government.

In forty-eight states, purchasing a Tesla automobile is restricted or even illegal. Why? Because Tesla doesn't use dealers.

Dell Computer built their entire business on the direct-to-consumer model and no one had any issue with that. Probably the most successful retail outlet of the last decade was Apple selling direct to customers in their superstores. Again, no issues.

So why the pushback against Tesla?

The laws in this space were created originally to protect franchise dealers of automakers like Ford, GM, and Chrysler. (Today, Ford or Chevy couldn't open a store in LA, even if they wanted to.) Of course, Tesla has a new business model and had no existing dealers to "protect." So what's the problem?

Those existing dealers for the legacy automakers. They like the system just the way it is and don't want to give their manufacturers any ideas. They're trying to prevent disruption through legislation.

As I'm writing this, the state of Utah is trying to shut down Zenefits, a new start-up that offers a cloud-based dashboard to

HR departments. The dashboard helps manage HR functions like hiring, benefits, and payroll. Zenefits offers the dashboard for free and makes money from insurance commissions if companies opt to sign over management of their insurance to the company.

It appears the other insurance agents aren't particularly fond of competing against free, so like other disrupted industries, they've lobbied their government representatives to ban Zenefits. Utah's insurance commissioner accused the company of violating the state's rebates and inducement law by giving away its software for free.

A similar dynamic is taking place with websites like Airbnb, which offers homeowners the opportunity to rent out to short-term guests. In most locales, services like these are operating in the shadows, as governments haven't decided how to deal with them. But, of course, they're attracting some vocal critics, because the model could disrupt real estate and hotels.

Probably the most visible example of this clash between disruptive models and archaic laws is Uber. In many cities, cab companies are lobbying local governments to protect their monopoly by banning ride-sharing apps.

You've heard the arguments: drivers aren't vetted, vehicles aren't inspected, the government hasn't sanctioned them, taxi drivers have paid the requisite permits and medallion fees, passengers will be at risk, etc.

That's the way we've thought about the taxi business (and protecting consumers) for decades. But is that thinking still serving us today?

If I call a taxi in Miami, I'll get a beat-up old car, and it's a crapshoot if it will have a working air-conditioner, accept credit cards, or show up within twenty minutes. If I call one in San

Diego, the cab will be newer and arrive within ten minutes, but 40 percent of the time when I offer my credit card, the driver will respond with, "You don't have cash?"

When I hail an Uber car in either city, the driver will be waiting in front before I get down in the elevator. The cars are always new and clean. The drivers are always friendly because they know the app gives the customer an opportunity to rate them after every hire. The charge and tip are automatically billed to my credit card, saving me time and making my bookkeeping and tax receipts seamless.

As I'm writing this, Paris is one of the cities in the throes of a taxi/Uber war. Taxi drivers there have been staging protests by parking their cabs in the streets during rush hour, causing horrendous gridlock. Like cab drivers in many other markets, they want Uber banned to "protect consumers."

What's the reality?

I'm a frequent visitor to Paris and can testify that it is notoriously under-taxied with old, filthy cabs. If you want to get across the city in the evening in a timely manner, your only option is to take the Metro, with riders packed in a grubby car. The idea of calling a taxi company for a pickup is virtually nonexistent there, and hailing a cab on the street often involves wait times of twenty to forty minutes. Once I almost missed my flight home because it took over an hour to hail a taxi in the Marais district. So naturally, on my last trip there, I opted for Uber.

The driver showed up within minutes in a meticulously clean, new Mercedes, with a daily newspaper and bottled water for me. The dinner companions I was meeting charted my progress until arrival. The driver was dressed sharp, very friendly, and spoke three languages. I got to dinner in half the normal time for roughly the same price.

I was so impressed I booked him to take me to the airport the next morning. He showed up with a bag of fresh, warm croissants for me. Game over.

The taxi model is built on a system of selling permits or medallions for huge fees, ensuring that there are more customers than cabs. But that whole monopoly model breaks down when you have free market competition.

Whether we are talking taxis, car manufacturers, Zenefits, Airbnb, or dozens of other start-ups, the situation is the same: Industries are being revolutionized by innovators with better business models, and the incumbents in the space are trying to use government to hobble or eliminate the competition. And it forces us to ask the question of whether this is really the highest good for consumers.

The disruptive times we're entering now will require a dramatically higher level of thinking about governance. We have to kill the meme that governments create jobs and prosperity. They don't. At best, government can facilitate prosperity; most times they simply squander it. And regardless of what governments do or don't do, the free market recognizes and responds to opportunities earlier, moves faster to solve problems, and develops more audacious innovation. The next decade will produce countless millionaires who thought "I can do what the government does, only better." If you don't believe me, ask UPS and FedEx.

BE LIKE WATER

Of course, the chapter title comes from Bruce Lee, the legendary martial artist, poet, and philosopher. While he has been quoted often, few actually understand what Lee meant by those words, and the story of how the expression came about.

I want to focus on it here because the story holds a very important lesson for how we have to change the way we think.

The story begins when Lee was still training with Professor Yip Man, head of the wing chun school of kung fu, the only formal martial arts training Lee ever received. During the training, Yip Man repeatedly came up to Lee and said, "Loong, relax and calm your mind. Forget about yourself and follow the opponent's movements. Let your mind, the basic reality, do the counter-movement without any interfering deliberation. Above all, learn the art of detachment."

These were abstract concepts to the young Lee, and he experienced great frustration and consternation. He would tell himself to relax but instinctively do something to contradict his will. Seeing his anxiety, Yip Man returned again and said, "Loong, preserve yourself by following the natural bend of things and don't interfere. Remember to never assert yourself against nature; never be in frontal opposition to any problem, but control it by swinging with it." After a time, the instructor told his young student to stop practicing for a week, go home, get away from the routines, and reflect.

Lee spent a week practicing and meditating, but felt no closer to what he was seeking. In an attempt to clear his mind, he went out sailing by himself on a junk in the Hong Kong harbor. Here's what happened next, in Lee's own words from his essay "A Moment of Understanding":

On the sea I thought of all my past training and got mad at myself and punched the water! Right then—at that moment—a thought suddenly struck me; was not the water the very essence of gung fu? Hadn't the water just now illustrated to me the principle of gung fu? I struck it, but it did not suffer hurt. Again I struck it with all my might—yet it was not wounded! I then tried to grasp a handful of it, but this proved impossible. This water, the softest substance in the world, which could be contained in the smallest jar, only seemed weak. In reality, it could penetrate the hardest substance in the world. That was it! I wanted to be like the nature of water.

Suddenly a bird flew by and cast its reflection on the water. Right then as I was absorbing myself with the lessons of the water, another mystic sense of hidden meaning revealed itself to me; should not the thoughts and emotions I had when in front of an opponent pass like the reflection of the bird flying over the water? That was exactly what Professor Yip meant by being detached—not being without emotion or feeling, but being one in whom feeling was not sticky or blocked. Therefore, in order to control myself, I must first accept myself by going with and not against my nature.

After his epiphany, Lee just lay there and let the boat drift freely, feeling united with Tao. He possessed a feeling in which opposition had become mutually cooperative instead of mutually exclusive, and he lost all feeling of conflict in his mind.

That experience on the water was a breakthrough moment for him and became a defining concept later in life when Lee went on to found jeet kune do. And that is where we can learn much about how we can best respond to challenges, setbacks, and the mindset necessary for Mad Genius. Because here's the thing:

At some point in your quest for Mad Genius you're going to be stuck in conventional thinking caused by your existing beliefs and programming. Or you'll finally break from that but will encounter clients, coworkers, or bosses who are afraid of big ideas. They will be armed with feasibility studies, committees, or long-standing corporate culture of why bold, daring, and imaginative things simply cannot be done.

It is times such as these that you must be like water. Bend, adapt, reshape, and reform. Find new directions or different levels. You have to stop trying to assert yourself with frontal opposition against nature, but bend with it.

Sometimes you don't have a choice in the events that happen to you. But you always have the choice in how you respond to those events.

TAP INTO
THE POWER OF THE
MASTERMIND

Bob Negen has been an entrepreneur for pretty much his whole life. He ran his own retail businesses for years, and nowadays he and his wife, Susan, have a very successful practice coaching other retailers on how to be successful. Bob is a big believer in the power of the mastermind. He told me:

> I've concluded that the foundation for my creativity comes from long, hard-earned experience, but the spark that brings out my genius is the energy and feedback I get from the people I'm serving when I'm speaking or coaching.
>
> Our marketing techniques for small, independent retailers are the most innovative and effective anywhere. Period. But someone else was always the spark that brought them to light. Something someone else said or asked was always the catalyst to every original strategy, tactic, or technique.

The Negens are participants in a mastermind group of Internet marketers that I'm a member of. We all relish the creative spark that comes from getting bright minds together to create a more powerful mastermind.

The most famous proponent of the mastermind is probably Napoleon Hill. I'm a member of several informal mastermind groups with some bright friends, and the formal one I'm in with the Negens. I swear by these groups, but I am also a big believer in another piece of advice from Hill, not as well known:

The first mastermind alliance you must form is with yourself.

We all have duality, both positive and negative. And the older most people get, the more they are drawn to the negative side. This is because the vast majority of subliminal programming and mind viruses circling the globe today are of the negative and limiting variety.

So when you are offered an opportunity, you have two choices:

A. Wow, I could crush with this.
B. That works for other people, but it would never work for me.

When you are facing a serious threat from a competitor:

A. OK, we're going to have to get better, but we can beat this.
B. I wonder if we'll make it.

When a business venture is failing:

A. What lesson can I take from this to win the next time?

B. I knew it would fail. You have to have money to make money.

Every one of us has a default setting. It is the mental attitude that determines whether we automatically go positive or go negative.

There is a side of you that wants to wallow in victimhood and validate every setback as preordained. You absolve yourself of responsibility, convince yourself that while you gave it your best effort, it was just not meant to be.

There is another side of you that has faith and knows that no is never the answer. This side simply does not recognize defeat as anything but a temporary setback, a growing experience, and an opportunity to learn and modify.

It is this second side of you that creates greatness and does epic things. That is the side of you that you must nurture. Get in touch with that side of you and make that your first mastermind alliance.

GET WET!

Actor David Lawrence XVII, who is also a serial entrepreneur, fuels his creative genius the old-fashioned way: in the shower. He told me:

> For me, when it comes to creative thinking, and especially when I'm having difficulty wrapping my brain around something, there is nothing in the world like taking a shower.
>
> I've had insanely great insights, created new and profitable products, solved thorny pricing and branding issues, even created whole new businesses by stepping in the shower and letting the isolation, the constant thrumming of the water, the repetitious and familiar moves of getting clean wash the distractions of the world away and allow my mind to open up and the breakthroughs to happen.
>
> And apparently others are in on this too. Google 'shower creative thinking' and you get over two million relevant results.

NURTURING YOUR INNER ARTIST

In a December 2013 article in *Forbes* magazine on fostering creativity, Alex Knapp wrote, "And if you want to foster those creative, problem solving skills, the solution isn't learning to code—it's learning to paint. Or play an instrument. Or write poetry. Or sculpt. The field doesn't matter: the key thing is that if you want to foster your own innovative creativity, the best way to do it is to seriously pursue an artistic endeavor."

Entrepreneurs have no need for the science versus art debate. We know that entrepreneurial thinking requires both.

Albert Einstein said that if he weren't a physicist, he would probably have been a musician. There are a lot of similarities in the creative process—whether you are composing an opera, scientifically testing a hypothesis, or creating the tag line for your new product.

Creative people aren't necessarily those who are the best educated or possess the highest IQs. In fact, because of the way the formal education system is designed, it often squelches creativity. Much of what is taught in schools and universities today is simply memorization, which inhibits creativity. And the way math and other sciences are often taught also focuses only on the logical side, to the detriment of creative thinking.

We take beautiful, bright five-year-olds—full of creativity— and tell them to sit up straight at their desks, not talk, and raise their hand when they want to go to the bathroom. Eventually the school system beats their creativity into submission.

Cherish your visions, nourish your creativity, and sow your ideals. Find the magic in your imagination.

I know you're busy: Bills to pay, housework to finish, rush hour to get through, your job to do. I get all that. But find time to be a philosopher, photographer, writer, sculptor, musician, dancer, or poet. Feed the creative energy in you and watch a new world open up for you. It's no accident that creative geniuses like Jared Leto, Harry Connick Jr., and Jennifer Hudson excel in different disciplines.

For entrepreneurs, the activity that requires the most creativity is innovation. All great entrepreneurs (and all managers and organizational leaders who think like entrepreneurs) face the need to innovate. Innovation is where the greatest breakthroughs live because we're getting away from what already is and creating what will be.

Entrepreneur and social media evangelist Gary Vaynerchuk thinks of innovation as a religion. In a December 9, 2013, post, he wrote, "It's not a method, it's a mindset. Everybody's looking for tactics, but it's more about religion. So the reason my team and I stay ahead is that we're built to stay ahead. We value the ROI that comes from the time we spend researching and pondering and debating and playing. We view that as a necessity. I don't think a lot of people consciously *value* oxygen, but you need it to stay alive. That is how I look at innovation."

CREATIVITY FROM LOGIC

Lest you think Mad Genius is all lava lamps, mood rings, and burning incense, logic most definitely plays an important role.

I'm writing this manifesto from my new apartment in downtown San Diego. Looking out my office window, I can watch the ongoing construction of a new office building nearby. It's a huge structure, taking up almost the entire block. Every week or two they have to lay another concrete floor for the parking garage. Now the interesting thing about that is when you float a concrete floor, you have to do the entire thing at one time.

With big projects in urban areas, a job like this poses quite a challenge. To pour that floor, the construction company has to deal with lane closures, rush hour traffic, government permits, weather, and union rules, to name just a few. Which is why I spent more than an hour or two, standing transfixed at my window, watching the process.

On Tuesday they had closed three lanes on 10th Avenue to park a huge, monster machine that would deliver the concrete to the next floor about to be laid. On Wednesday at 8 a.m. the process started when ten cement trucks rumbled up. Two immediately backed up to the monster machine, and one began dumping concrete into its belly. Two more trucks pulled in front of the two unloading, one behind the other, forming a queue. The other six trucks waited behind the machine. One guy directed traffic at the start of the block, another guy in the middle, and a third at the end. Two guys with push brooms kept the street clean. Twenty-five to thirty men worked on the rebar, smoothing the concrete as it was unloaded from the monster.

It took about six minutes for the first truck to empty its concrete. Traffic worker two stopped traffic so it could depart. The back truck of the two waiting reversed into the spot just vacated by the empty truck. Then the front truck backed up one spot, ready to replace the second truck now emptying its load. The first truck from the six in back took its place in front of the queue. The two guys with brooms cleaned up. Six minutes later, the second truck left and the whole process repeated itself. Another truck appeared at the end of the queue. This happened again every six minutes without stop, all day long.

At four o'clock workers started erecting spotlights to illuminate the corner of the floor that hadn't been finished. Every six minutes the dance repeated. At 4:30, the last truck emptied its load and departed, just as rush hour began. The twenty-five to thirty guys on the floor worked another two hours under the lights, as the sun set, smoothing out the concrete.

Being on the twenty-second floor, I had a perfect seat for the performance. You could bring in Debbie Allen, Nappytabs, or Travis Wall, and they couldn't choreograph a more stunning dance routine.

It's the same when you go to the Atlanta airport and watch the beehive of activity from airplanes, luggage carts, and cargo platforms. The synchronization requires logic that is poetic to get all the right people, luggage, and crews to the right planes.

Logistical challenges like this—which we face in business all the time—require a precise logical approach. But you still must be creative to find the logical solution.

FAIL MORE

One major thing that separates a successful entrepreneur from those who are not successful is their willingness to fail. Successful people fail all the time. We fail our way to success. We fail where others have succeeded, sure, but more importantly, we fail where no one else has thought to try.

I said earlier the opposite of success is not failure but mediocrity. Failure is simply part of the success process. It teaches you lessons, develops your character, and allows you to modify your approach to find the right way to reach greatness.

Remember, the entrepreneur who doesn't make mistakes doesn't make anything.

BE "THE ONE"

For many of you, it isn't a breakthrough product or service you're looking for. You already have an amazing one and your challenge is how to create marketing that makes it stand out from the crowd. Some products or businesses become breakthroughs simply because they cut through the noise and make a splash in the marketplace. When everyone is zigging, you need to be zagging.

Most business speakers customize their speech to the client, do pre-event research, attend the cocktail reception beforehand, and show up in the appropriate corporate attire. Except Larry Winget, who will rock up to the platform in a loud shirt, jeans, and cowboy boots. He has no interest in pre-event research, won't attend your social event, and he'll deliver the exact same speech he gives everyone else.

Most consultants submit thirty-page proposals, keep from making waves, and chase after payment. Alan Weiss refuses to do proposals, gets in his clients' faces, and demands payment upfront. In full.

I work out at a big gym that has all the usual safety requirements. There's a guy I see working out three or four times a week who looks like a walking phone booth. (Under-thirty readers: Google "phone booth.") He's inked from head to foot. And I mean literally. His head is shaved, and he has gnarly tats all over his skull.

This guy doesn't mess with no pansy-boy machines. He mostly does free weights, doing three-hundred-pound clean and jerks, skull crushers, and bicep curls with ninety-five-pound dumbbells. Every time I have ever seen the man, he is wearing flip-flops. And no one ever tells Tat-Dude he has to be wearing goddamned shoes.

So how do you take what Winget, Weiss, or Tat-Dude does and apply it in your own space?

There are burger chains and then there's In-N-Out Burger.

There are female vocalists and then there's Aretha.

There are doughnut shops and then there's Krispy Kreme.

There are movie directors and then there's Martin Scorsese.

There are hardware chains and then there's Ace Hardware.

There are computer companies and then there's Apple.

There are branding, marketing, brainstorming, or product development meetings and then there's Mad Genius.

CHANGE YOUR
THOUGHT PATTERNS

The average person repeats thousands of the same thoughts, day after day. Research has shown that these actually follow the same pattern and create ruts in the neural pathways of your brain. The more you disrupt these patterns and jump out from these ruts, the better chance you have to tap into your Mad Genius.

Switch the wrist you wear your watch on, try texting with your nondominant hand, or drive a different way home from work. You'll create new neural patterns in your brain.

Creative people are:

- Self-motivated
- Independent
- Delighted by novelty
- Risk takers
- Tolerant of ambiguity
- Deeply involved in their work
- Avid readers
- World travelers

These characteristics provide creative people with a very rich diet of stimulation, variety, and diverse experiences. They are exposed to a steady stream of new opinions, languages, cultures, and attitudes. They see a much broader spectrum of society, people in general, and the world. They see the same challenge handled in many different ways, which opens up the mind to problem solving, lateral thinking, and innovation.

When is the last time you really questioned your core foundational beliefs about money, relationships, religion, or government?

Do you solve Sudoku puzzles, word games, brainteasers, and other things to stimulate your mental capacity? Do you watch or listen to commentators who have opposing political viewpoints from your own? Is your inner circle all people who agree with you, or does it reflect diversity of opinion?

Read book series like Harry Potter and Lord of the Rings. Go to science fiction movies like *The Matrix* and *Inception*. Listen to a different genre of music than you normally do. Study the way Aaron Sorkin crafts dialogue or Bill Simmons writes about sports.

Go out for dinner and coffee with people whose hobbies, backgrounds, and jobs are dissimilar to yours. Read a foreign magazine occasionally. Take a college course in something you know nothing about. Go to Wikipedia and hit the "Random Article" link a dozen times.

One of the reasons I conduct so many mastermind sessions and leadership retreats in Las Vegas is so that I can take the participants to see a performance by Cirque du Soleil.

Being so immersed in self-development, I can't experience a Cirque show without seeing all the parallels to success and achievement. Because at the end of the day, the Cirque shows are really about the triumph of the human spirit.

They are about possibilities and potential, faith and belief. They will wake you up to the hidden child and artistic genius you may have lost touch with.

Afraid that the achievement you're striving for is impossible? Check out some of the acrobatic feats in the show and you will have a new and bigger view of possibility.

Feeling like your creative genius is blocked? Watch the first five minutes of the show and your creativity will be energized like you stuck your finger in a light socket.

Need some motivation to get in shape? Take one look at the bodies of some of those performers and you will drop that doughnut like it's radioactive.

The lighting, costumes, music, staging, and performances are such artistic genius—no one can be exposed to them without having their own genius inspired. Experiences like these disrupt stale thought patterns and help develop new ones. Virtually any Cirque show will unleash your imagination, nurture your creativity, and expand your vision. You will believe in the power of your genius again.

TAKE A
SABBATICAL

This very manifesto is coming to you live and in color from my own sabbatical. (Although by the time you're actually reading it, I will have rejoined the real world.) For me this sabbatical has been the most brilliant experience I've ever gone through. It has jump-started my creativity in wondrous and profuse ways. You, too, might be at a point in your life or career where a sabbatical is right for you.

First, make sure you know what a sabbatical is and why you're doing it. Many people think a sabbatical is like a long vacation, but that's not accurate. Sabbaticals are really about learning and growing. I modeled my sabbatical on the concept of people who take a year off to do post-graduate work at Oxford University. (And since Oxford would never accept a vagabond like me, I created my own learning program.)

My objective was a high-intensity, concentrated program of self-development and personal growth. Some days I read three books; other days I watch fifteen TED videos. Every day I do cardio exercise and weight training, because no one can tap their true mental potential if they're not well physically. Not only have I gotten in the best shape of my life and become wiser, but I really feel this opened up many new channels for my creativity.

Another consideration is the finances. It really works best when you have the money thing out of the way. If you're not there yet, set a goal for when you could take a sabbatical and work toward that.

The other issue to think about is how to know when you're done. In my case I left it open-ended: I wanted to travel, learn a language or two, finish this manifesto, create an online learning platform, and really accelerate my own education. You could do something like that or you could confine it to a specific time frame like six months or a year.

You can't wait until your inbox is empty to focus on the big things. Your inbox will never be empty, but your well of Mad Genius will be.

GET OUT OF BED
EARLIER

On this sabbatical I can wake up anytime I want. Yet most days I'm up at 5 a.m. There is something inherently spiritual about the early morning hours. Most of the world is asleep and it's a great time for reading, writing, meditating, and other activities that nourish your Mad Genius.

READ THE FEARSOME FOURSOME

There are four books that are breathtaking in the creative energy they offer you—three by Steven Pressfield and another from Seth Godin. Every musician, writer, dancer, sculptor, and especially entrepreneur should read them.

They are *The War of Art*, *Turning Pro*, and *Do the Work* by Pressfield, and *The Icarus Deception* by Godin. I hope you've already read each of these great works.

Read them again. In order. In one weekend. It will be an orgy of creative stimulation that will leave you fired up and breathless to get back to your own artistic endeavors.

SCHEDULE
THINKING TIME

There may be no better way to innovate, think creatively, or brainstorm exciting new possibilities than spending time in quiet reflection. And in today's hectic world, you probably need to schedule that time.

Every week make it a point to block off at least forty-five minutes in your schedule just for thinking. Really.

PLAY THE
"WHAT IF" GAME

Bend reality and create new rules to think by. Propose the wildest, most outrageous, and preposterous things you can imagine. They do not have to be practical, possible, or even plausible. For a time, operate in a world where there are no rules, etiquette, laws, or standards. You escape the physical limitations of the world to see what your ultimate solution would be. Once you shrug off the physical limitations, your inspired thinking will be boundless.

A great way to stimulate creative thinking is by asking "what if" questions like:

- If it were possible, how could it be done?
- What if we started over from scratch and did it another way?
- What if we manufactured it under water?
- What if there were no gravity?
- What if money were no object?
- How would a five-year-old approach this problem?
- What if we manufactured it in the dark?
- What if we assembled it in subzero temperatures?
- What if we had to get it done in twenty-four hours?

Don't edit or evaluate answers at first, just allow the brain-storming process to unfold. Only after you have finished asking and answering your questions should you look back at the ideas you have generated. Then look for ways in which all or part of these ideas could be made practical.

Think of the benefits you could gain by using a new idea and work out how you can achieve the same thing in reality. How could you modify the suggested solution to make it work? What changes in the world would you need to make that idea possible, and how can you make those changes happen?

EXTRAPOLATE

Another useful technique is analogy thinking. Take an existing situation and apply it in a totally different context. Looking at what happens in unrelated industries can provide brilliant insights and inspiration into your own.

For example, I once took the concept from a commercial promoting a radio station and applied it in a display ad for a hair styling salon I owned. Often you can take a practice that is used in the oil exploration business and apply it in the healthcare industry. Or vice versa.

Creativity expert Victoria Labalme harnesses her years of show business experience to teach experts, entrepreneurs, and executives how to communicate better. She often uses analogy thinking with her clients to produce powerful results. Labalme told me:

> Many think they're not "creative." We've heard that before from studies about adults versus children. But creativity is not some hocus-pocus, voodoo talent reserved for the elite. Rather, it's a matter of tapping into what you already have and combining your unique interests and gifts in a new way.
>
> You're leading a company now but were the drummer for your college rock band? Cool. Why not use drumming as an analogy in your next internal presentation? Talk about the importance of rhythm, coordination, and focus.

You're a strategic planning specialist who is a fan of Letterman and comedy? Why not start your meeting with a Top Ten List?

Let's say you're a financial analyst whose daughter is a jump-roping whiz. Perfect. Use jump roping as a metaphor to address the importance of timing when entering and exiting the market . . . planning your moves carefully so you don't trip and get whacked by the rope. You get the idea.

Believe it or not, these are all examples from my clients. And they work. Theirs are the presentations that stand out, the ones that people remember long after the conference.

Creativity requires courage: courage to explore ideas and instincts no matter how quirky they may be; to create a connection between two seemingly disparate elements; courage to put it out in the world.

And even if it's not great out of the gate, the attempt will certainly be what I call "the idea that will lead to the idea."

And that idea will spur new ones. Very few people get it right the first time. But one thing's for sure. If you don't give it a shot, if you continue to do what everyone else in your field, industry, and cul-de-sac always does, you will never fulfill the full expression of who you are truly meant to be.

MAKE LOVE WITH THE LIGHTS ON

In the kitchen. On the counter.

GO BACK
TO SCHOOL

Figuratively or literally. My sabbatical has been a wonderful opportunity for me to work on me. But even without going on a sabbatical, you can always schedule time for self-development.

Find some seminars, workshops, or conventions that will challenge your thinking and help you develop new skills. My practice is to always schedule at least two events a year where I am not a presenter but attend only as a student.

GET YOUR JERSEY
BURNED

We'll assume you already have customers, even fans. Maybe even a tribe of devotees who appreciate your work and follow you. But how much passion are you really creating?

Remember back when basketball superstar LeBron James made his decision to go from Cleveland to Miami? The Cleveland fans were tearing down his posters and burning his jerseys in effigy. Probably you want to never be reviled and despised like that.

But maybe you should.

The reason LeBron created such vehement reactions both positive and negative is because he was the best basketball player in the world at that time. People loved him and others loved to hate him. That means he matters. He's relevant. He's doing amazing things.

Athletes change sports teams all the time. If they're mediocre, no one cares. If they're good, fans get upset. If they're great, people are passionate enough to burn their jerseys, hire sky writers, or perform some other public act to show their anguish and agony.

If you want to be a thought leader, market leader, or change the world—you have to give up the need to be liked. Telling people what they want to hear makes you popular. Telling people what they *need* to hear makes you relevant, empowering, and significant.

Don't pander to the masses. Speak to the people you really want to reach and be honest. Challenge them to do more and become better. And know that if you're not attracting some haters—you're probably not doing something significant. So that leads us to a fascinating question for you . . .

Would they burn your jersey?

HAVE AT LEAST ONE PERSON
WHO WILL CALL YOU
ON YOUR SHIT

Michael Jackson and Amy Winehouse were creative geniuses. Charlie Sheen is too. But even geniuses need someone who can tell them when they are off the rails. You need a couple people in your life who love you, tell you the truth, and will call you on your shit.

It's vital to know that these are people who really want the best for you and aren't damping you down out of jealousy or limiting beliefs. Find at least one person you trust in this way and bounce ideas off them.

Sometimes your work is ahead of its time. Sometimes it's so brilliant others will have difficulty getting it. And sometimes it's just shit. Have people in your life who are qualified to know the difference and love you enough to tell you the truth.

BREAK OUT
THE SIMPLE STICK

In his book *Insanely Simple*, author Ken Segall relates incident after incident when Steve Jobs would disrupt a creative process at Apple by beating them with "the simple stick."

There's a fascinating story about when Mike Evangelist, the director of product development at Apple, went to the initial development meeting for the iDVD app. Mike showed up armed with all kinds of slides, screen shots, and explanations his committee had developed to demonstrate how the interface would work.

What happened instead shocked him. Jobs strode into the room, ignored all their preparation, and walked up to the whiteboard.

"Here's the new application," he said. "It's got one window. You drag your video into the window. Then you click the button that says 'Burn.' That's it. That's what we're going to make."

Mike and his team were dumbfounded. But, of course, that's the app that Apple eventually created. Their magic always was and is simplicity. If the project or concept you're working on has started to creep into complexity, it may be time to break out the simple stick.

BE BALLSY

When you're working in areas like marketing and branding, having the guts to do something provocative, gutsy, or downright confrontational will often cut through the clutter and produce breakthrough results.

The best stand-up comedians say what everyone is thinking but is afraid to say. The best branding works the same way. Say what everyone else is thinking, but no one has the guts to say out loud.

One of my consulting clients was a direct sales company having difficulty attracting new distributors. They were running ads in the back of business publications, along with a bunch of other advertisers, eight on a page, each competing for attention.

I increased their response percentage by more than 10,000 percent by creating an ad with the headline "Are You a Schmuck?" It went on to make fun of the idea of spending anywhere from $30,000 to $1 million on a franchise, to arguably buy yourself a minimum wage job wearing a paper hat.

The magazine did receive a few complaints and pulled the ad, but only after we had three print runs and more leads than the company could possibly handle.

Another client was a salon owned by a gay stylist that provided hair replacement systems for men. They were advertising in a publication for gay men. So naturally I created a new ad with this headline and subhead:

YOU'RE BALD, UGLY, AND QUEER . . .
Fortunately, We Can Fix the First Two

As with the schmuck ad, I warned my client that he might get some blowback, but I thought it was worth the risk. The result surprised even me. Not a single complaint, sales went through the roof, and even prospects who didn't buy called or stopped by his shop to say how funny they thought the ad was.

In my own business, I was promoting a three-day seminar with a pretty hefty price tag. And competing against dozens of other companies and promoters offering workshops, seminars, and boot camps. So I created a direct mail campaign that included a bulky envelope containing an adult diaper. The basis of the copy platform was how once they attended the seminar and saw the response rates we were getting with my marketing strategies, they were going to crap their pants. We sold out the event.

And speaking of seminars, guess what exciting new marketing strategy I'm employing to sell out events these days?

Yes, we make a Facebook page, build an email list, use social media, all the usual stuff. But the big differentiator is using good old-fashioned direct mail.

Because nobody else is doing it.

They all think direct mail is dead and crow about how much money they're saving on printing and postage. So often my mailings are the only ones in the prospect's mailbox.

I've done mailings that included $100 bills to grab important prospects' attention, used shiny foil envelopes, and even hired Brownie troops to hand address each envelope in crayon.

I've done mailings where the first page is missing and the top page says something like:

Page 2

just for you. So if you're interested in the free car, profit sharing, and award trips I mentioned on page one, you must call me at 1-800-XXX-XXXX within 24 hours.

You'd be amazed how many people call, demanding to know what page one was. And when we fess up and tell them we intentionally left it out to get their attention, most get a big kick out of it.

One of my all-time favorite techniques was renting a mailing list for two mailings. I mailed the first sales letter and got a certain percentage of responses who bought. We culled those names from the list and mailed the same offer again to the remaining people. Only this time (hiring the Brownies again), we crumpled up the letters, flattened them out, and wrote with a red sharpie at the top, "Please DON'T throw this away again!"

This usually boosts the original response rate by another 30 to 40 percent. (And yes, you do get one or two hysterical people who threaten to call the police because they really believe you dug through their garbage.) There's a reason it's called *Mad* Genius.

Obviously this kind of in-your-face approach doesn't work for all markets. But it will work in a lot more than most people think. When everyone else is zigging, you want to be zagging.

MIND MAPPING

One of the all-time greatest techniques for getting creative juices flowing and really thinking off the chain is mind mapping. This is a process that is inherently creative, and all it requires is a pen and paper (and your open mind).

Instead of thinking laterally, which is the way most people approach an idea, you explore and expand an idea in many different directions without a logical pattern. This allows you to come up with new and fresh perspectives that you couldn't otherwise. Here are some suggestions:

Connect the dots: Use lines, arrows, shapes, colors, and codes to indicate relationships and connections between ideas.

Fill the page: Start with a central image or word to focus the eye and brain and trigger associations. Then let one idea lead to another.

Be clear: Print key words, with only one word on a line.

Create your own style: These are guidelines not rules. Discover what works best for you.

THE SCAMPER TECHNIQUE

Here's a technique from Bob Eberle and Alex Osborne that is used to develop more creativity in the workplace. It's a helpful technique for exploring possible solutions to a challenge.

SCAMPER is an acronym for the seven different ways you can view an idea. This process might seem silly at first, but it's the kind of technique that lets bold, daring, and imaginative ideas come forth.

Remember, creativity is like a muscle; it can be strengthened with exercise. Here's the SCAMPER technique broken down:

Substitute

Combine

Adapt

Modify

Put to other uses

Eliminate

Reverse/rearrange

An example of SCAMPER using an umbrella:

Substitute: Use a plastic bag stretched over a wire coat hanger.

Combine: Add a radio and digital clock to the handle.

Adapt: Make it useful for joggers by attaching it to the body.

Modify: Make it big enough to cover several people at once.

Put to other uses: Use the tip for making holes or picking up litter.

Eliminate: Take away the metal spokes that are always bending.

Reverse/rearrange: Have the umbrella fold up instead of down to catch the water.

Whether you are looking to redesign a product, create a new market, or rebrand a longtime institution, the SCAMPER technique is a great way to get your lateral thinking process engaged.

START BEHAVING LIKE A CHILD!

One of the best and most creative ways to approach any situation that's in need of innovation is to think like a five-year-old. That is the point in most people's lives when they were at their peak creative state, before it was beaten out of them.

Children at that age don't concern themselves with things like government regulations, social etiquette, or accepted practices. They just focus on what they want to accomplish and how it can be done.

Yes, the Panama Canal, Great Wall of China, and the Pyramids are breathtaking. But do you have a clue how astounding a can opener is? Kids have a sense of wonder about the entire world. Elevators are mysterious, escalators are amazing, and airplanes are magic.

When you seem stuck on a challenge, stop seeing it through your grown-up eyes and try to picture it as a kid might. Make yourself a peanut butter and jelly sandwich, drink some chocolate milk, go outside, and play on a swing for a while.

BREAK
THE RULES

If you want to write a song, there are certain structures to follow. Unless you decide to break them all and create something brilliant like Ed Sheeran does.

If you want to produce a popular television show, be mindful of scale, number of characters, and the limitations of the small screen. Unless you want to produce *Game of Thrones*, the most successful television show in the world.

If you want to sell books, do it the way it's been working for at least two hundred years. Unless you want to create something like Amazon.

If you're going to compose an opera, you have to do it keeping in mind the limitations of the human voice. Unless you're Wagner and want to make something that will still be mesmerizing people centuries later.

If you want to create a fantasy blockbuster, make sure to ground it in a believable reality. Unless you want to produce something epic like Harry Potter, *DUNE*, or *Interstellar*.

If you're going to manufacture a utilitarian product like a

telephone, stick to the basic functionality. Unless you want to create the iPhone.

When it comes to rules, here's the only one that counts:

Know the rules, and be willing to break the rules—as long as you know why you're breaking them.

STOP SETTLING

You see that a competitor has a strong market share, so you decide to just cede the space to them.

No one's ever done it before, so you decide it's better not to attempt it.

You launch your cutting edge, innovative product, but market it with boring, conventional advertising because that seems normal.

You build a cookie-cutter website because all the other companies in your industry do it that way.

Stop it. That's the way the herd thinks, but that kind of thinking won't take you to where you want to be.

I wrote *Risky Is the New Safe* and now this manifesto because I knew that for most people and companies, the biggest obstacle they face is thinking it is safe to play it safe. And nothing could be further from the truth. The rules have changed, and playing it safe is actually the riskiest thing you can do today.

Please. Stop playing it safe and take a risk, because that's where the breakthroughs live. Stop living safe and start really living.

We are entering a decade that will offer exponentially accelerating growth, hyper-development, and disruption like the world has never witnessed before. The challenges you're about to face are more daunting than any you've ever experienced. They're more daunting than challenges *anyone* has ever experienced. Even if you're on top right now, the whole world could blow past you next month. The entrepreneurs and companies that succeed in the new economy will have to do so in wildly different ways than have ever been attempted before.

Leaders are born in turbulent times, and we are about to enter the most tumultuous time in human history. Not in fifty or seventy-five years, but now. Managers will need to learn how to manage through disorder—directing harmony amid chaos. Leadership will require more critical thinking, creativity, and risk taking than ever before. It will require Mad Genius.

We are going to need to find answers to the most perplexing questions and exhilarating possibilities humankind has ever faced.

The greatest hope for the world will not be found in political debate, more government regulations, or even higher learning. It's going to take a level of *thinking* higher than what we've been employing up to this point. And the people most likely to discover the answers we will desperately need are artists. Not just any artists, but the ones who proudly call themselves entrepreneurs. The past is behind; the future is beyond. It's time to make art.

We're about to enter the Age of the Entrepreneur.

Socialist philosophy and well-meaning entitlement programs have failed us. Collectivist bureaucracies, nanny-state control, and one-size-fits-all thinking must die. We must recognize that all prosperity is created in value-for-value equations. It is time to unleash the awesome power of free enterprise to restore balance to the equation.

We will still need compassion, empathy, and the arts. We need government to protect private property (especially intellectual), a court system to adjudicate disputes, and a military for our common defense. But we have to stop governments from penalizing success, choking innovation, and protecting the incumbents. We must merge art and enterprise to produce new thought processes.

Which brings us back to you, the entrepreneur—the challenges you will face and the extraordinary opportunities that will be hidden in those challenges. It's the perfect time to get your Mad Genius on, because

There has never been a better time to go from broke to multimillionaire—or even multibillionaire—than right now.

The critical thinkers who ask—and answer—the right questions will lead the companies and ventures that capture market share in the new space. They will be the visionaries who create bold new products, reinvent entire industries, blow up tired assumptions, and create thermofuckingnuclear.

What happens next?

It's only fair to warn you: Once you make this commitment to building something thermofuckingnuclear, you can be sure of certain things happening.

First, some people will doubt you. Others will ridicule you. Some may even attack you or your ideas. If you're really doing something thermofuckingnuclear, you're certain to have some haters.

Don't be worried about the doubters, cynics, or haters.

Be worried if you don't have any.

And know this: The haters don't really hate you. They hate themselves because they don't have the guts to do what you're doing.

But here's where it gets really, really scary.

Some of those people who will try to hold you back won't be readily apparent to you. They're the person in your committee meeting who just wants to play devil's advocate or the member of your church board who has done it that way for the last forty years. They're the VP in your Monday morning meeting who wants to point out how similar initiatives have failed or the investor who wants to know how fast they can get their investment back.

What they are really saying is "I'm afraid." And they are especially afraid of the people who are not afraid.

Don't hold any malice against these people because they don't have any malice for you. They honestly believe they know what's in your own best interest. And sometimes they actually do.

But most of the time, they bought the story of the MYSTE-RIOUS PEOPLE and assume they are protecting you from the bad things that happen to those who ignore the SECRET SYS-TEM THAT RUNS THE WORLD.

The people who buy that story live their lives in fear. Don't buy the story. Fear-based decisions produce fearful results. This is the moment to be bold. Don't wait for someone to appoint you. Make the first move.

It's not about being discovered, either. The world has discovered millions of superstars and forgot them in a matter of weeks, days, or even seconds. Mad Genius is about discovering yourself. Those who discover themselves are the people the world remembers.

Don't be one of the millions who coasted through their lives and died with their genius still left untapped. If you hoard your Mad Genius, it withers away. When you share it, it grows stronger.

Your Mad Genius might involve your job, it might be the job you have after this one, or it might be the thing you do outside of your job. One thing I know for certain: The universe won't give you your next assignment until you're overqualified for the one you're doing now.

Please. Stop playing small and step into your greatness.

Too many people in the business world are waiting for their fears to subside so they can act. So they never do.

Mad Genius entrepreneurs aren't fearless. We know there will always be fears. But we act in spite of those fears. (And often because of them.)

Be bold, daring, and imaginative, because the world needs Mad Genius right now. And *you* are just the person to provide it.

THE REAL CREDIT

Some authors sit down and channel ingenious books that make you see things differently. Unfortunately, I'm not one of those authors. Fortunately, though, I am a critical thinker who questions premises and is on an endless pursuit of thought-provoking big ideas. And when I find those big ideas, I present them for discussion and input from a collection of brilliant people I've assembled in my life. This manifesto is the result of that mastermind.

It can help you see your work (and even your life) in ways you never imagined before. The contributors include Dan Abelow, Tim Berry, Terry Brock, Bob Burg, Gina Carr, Joachim de Posada, Chuck Eglinton, JB Glossinger, Lisa Jimenez, Christopher Knight, Ian Percy, Nido Qubein, and Brian Short. Not to mention, a holy trinity of editors: Vicki McCown, Marian Lizzi, and Eric Nelson. They all gave most generously of their own Mad Genius, and I'm grateful for them. You will be too.

ABOUT THE AUTHOR

Randy Gage is a serial entrepreneur, angel investor, and thought-provoking critical thinker who will make you approach your business—and your life—in a whole new way. Randy's previous nine books have been translated into twenty-five languages. He has spoken to more than two million people across more than fifty countries and is a member of the CPAE Speaker Hall of Fame. When he is not prowling the platform or locked in his lonely writer's garret, you'll probably find him playing third base for a softball team somewhere. Find him at randygage.com or on Twitter @Randy_Gage with the hashtag #MadGenius.